MW01504872

A Litigator's Guide to Expert Witnesses

CECIL C. KUHNE III

GP|Solo

ABA General Practice, Solo & Small Firm Section

Cover design by ABA Publishing.

The materials contained herein represent the opinions and views of the authors and/or the editors, and should not be construed to be the views or opinions of the law firms or companies with whom such persons are in partnership with, associated with, or employed by, nor of the American Bar Association or the General Practice, Solo and Small Firm Section, unless adopted pursuant to the bylaws of the Association.

Nothing contained in this book is to be considered as the rendering of legal advice, either generally or in connection with any specific issue or case; nor do these materials purport to explain or interpret any specific bond or policy, or any provisions thereof, issued by any particular franchise company, or to render franchise or other professional advice. Readers are responsible for obtaining advice from their own lawyers or other professionals. This book and any forms and agreements herein are intended for educational and informational purposes only.

Printed in the United States of America

13 12 11 10   5 4 3 2

Library of Congress Cataloging-in-Publication Data

Kuhne, Cecil, 1952–
   A litigation guide to expert witnesses / by Cecil Kuhne.
     p. cm.
   Includes index.
   ISBN 978-1-59031-728-0
   1. Evidence, Expert—United States. 2. Examination of witnesses—United States.
3. Witnesses—United States. I. Title Association. Tort Trial and Insurance Practice Section.
II. Title.

   KF8961.K84   2006
   3447.73'67—dc22

                           2006028945

Discounts are available for books ordered in bulk. Special consideration is given to state bars, CLE programs, and other bar-related organizations. Inquire at Book Publishing, ABA Publishing, American Bar Association, 321 North Clark Street, Chicago, Illinois 60654-7598.

www.ababooks.org

Contents

CHAPTER 7
Presenting Experts   83

CHAPTER 8
Objecting to Experts   107

Introduction

The admission of expert witness testimony remains one of the most contentious, critical, and interesting aspects of modern-day litigation practice. And there is little sign that this tendency will abate anytime soon. The courts have struggled—and will continue to struggle—in their efforts to ensure reliable expert witness testimony without unduly invading the jury's province to independently assess the credibility of a particular witness.

The area is an important one. More than a few lawsuits have been won—and lost—solely on the performance of an expert witness. And many a case has settled before trial simply because a party recognized the capability of the expert retained by the other side. The advantages of well-honed expert testimony at trial are well-known, but expert witnesses can also be very critical in the early stages of litigation—assessing evidence, making suggestions for trial strategy, assembling critical documents, and all the other tasks involved in preparing for trial.

Attorneys who first think of hiring an expert when it is time to draft the witness list or reply to interrogatories will inevitably pay the price. And the price is a dear one. In all but the most routine cases the attorney must begin the search early on if the client's case is to be advanced as persuasively as possible.

The Supreme Court's decisions in *Daubert* and *Kumho Tire*— and their state court equivalents—of course changed the landscape of expert witnesses forever when they vested substantial discretion in trial judges to perform the mandatory gatekeeping functions. *Daubert* subjected the scientific testimony before it to a stringent analysis by asking the now-familiar regime of questions: (1) Was the opinion subjected to a peer-reviewed publication? (2) Does it have a known or knowable error rate? (3) Is it generally accepted in the relevant scientific field? and (4) Has it been tested or is it testable?

The subsequent case of *Kumho Tire* made clear that rigorous gatekeeping extended *beyond* scientific testimony and that defining specific tests for reliability was not practical in view of the wide range of expert testimony. As a result, courts have seen the need for increased flexibility when inquiring into the relevance and reliability of the testimony being evaluated.

▼▼▼▼▼

Daubert's Gatekeeping Role

We recognize that, in practice, a gatekeeping role for the judge, no matter how flexible, inevitably on occasion will prevent the jury from learning of authentic insights and innovations. That, nevertheless, is the balance that is struck by Rules of Evidence designed not for the exhaustive search for cosmic understanding but for the particularized resolution of legal disputes.

Daubert, 509 U.S. at 597.

The latest version of Federal Rule of Evidence 702 codified the rulings in *Daubert* and *Kumho Tire* and allow a qualified witness to testify only if (1) the testimony is based on sufficient facts or data, (2) the testimony is the product of reliable principles and methods, and (3) the witness has applied principles and methods reliably to the facts of the case.

This important evidentiary rule—and its state-court emula-
tions—has had two notable effects. It has to a large extent precluded
the "junk science" that was sometimes admitted prior to the recognized role of the court as a gatekeeper of expert testimony. But it has
also opened the door to the admissibility of evidence that was once
considered too novel but can now be shown to be reliable. The trial
courts retain considerable discretion in this regard, and the appellate courts are in turn highly deferential to those decisions.

▼▼▼▼▼

Judicial Discretion

[W]e conclude that the trial judge must have considerable leeway
in deciding in a particular case how to go about determining
whether particular expert testimony is reliable.

Kumho Tire, 526 U.S. at 152.

The liberalization of other federal evidentiary rules is likewise
important. Rule 703 allows the expert to rely on data or documents
that contain inadmissible hearsay or violate other exclusionary rules
as long as the reliance by the expert is reasonable. The rationale for
the rule is efficiency and trustworthiness of the expert, as checked by
an intense cross-examination from the other side.

Rule 704 specifically abolished the common-law "ultimate
issue" rule, which prohibited experts from testifying on ultimate
issues because it was believed that experts would thereby usurp
the province of the jury. This does not mean that an expert may
automatically give opinion testimony on ultimate issues, such as
whether the defendant was or was not negligent, but it does mean
that it will not be automatically excluded.

And Rule 705 abandoned the requirement that an expert disclose facts underlying the opinion as a prerequisite to admissibility of the opinion itself. Instead, the rule contemplates that the
underlying foundation for the expert's opinion will be elicited on
cross-examination, especially since the federal rules permit extensive discovery of an expert's opinions and the basis for those opinions. Rule 705 thus abolished the requirement of the hypothetical

question to the witness who does not have firsthand knowledge of the underlying facts.

Although the liberal approach of the Federal Rules of Evidence has led the majority of courts to allow a qualified expert to testify to virtually anything if a reliable and relevant methodology is shown, the rules do provide a framework by which the cross-examiner can effectively exclude or weaken the expert's opinion. The burden is therefore placed on the cross-examiner to uncover the basis of the expert witness' opinion, and exposing weaknesses dramatically affects the weight and credibility of the expert's testimony.

The practical importance of cross-examination is amply illustrated by the myriad cases in which a well-credentialed expert does poorly on cross-examination, causing the case to quickly unravel. These are precarious waters, and there is no substitute for meticulous preparation before trial by both the attorney and the expert.

The book you have before you strives to approach the subject in a logical fashion. The first half of the book sets forth the so-called legal side of things. Chapter 1 and 2 provide a general overview and description of the legal framework. Chapters 3, 4, and 5 are discussions of the critical Supreme Court decisions, discovery rules, and evidentiary rules dealing with expert witness testimony.

The second half of the book deals with more practical matters. Chapter 6 is devoted to the process of selecting an expert. Chapters 7 and 8 concern the presentation of experts and objections to your opponent's expert. Chapters 9, 10, and 11 discuss depositions, direct examination, and cross-examination.

The reader will note that federal rules and cases are used, rather than references to the myriad state jurisdictions. This has been done out of sheer necessity, and for the reason that most states have adopted statutes based on the federal model. Obviously, the practitioner cannot afford to neglect the particular statutes, rules, and cases of the venue at hand.

The material here is not intended to be a scholarly treatise containing reams of supporting citations. Such texts are well provided elsewhere. The goal is one of practicality and is born of a desire to provide useful handbook for the litigator who needs a quick refresher course when heading off to court, to a deposition, or to the library in a quest to argue for or against the admission of expert testimony.

Overview

1

THE WORLD OF EXPERT testimony is nothing if not diverse. Consider several situations that might occur in the daily lives of litigators:

Scenario 1: An experienced pilot crashes while flying his small single-engine plane on a perfectly clear day in West Texas. An equipment malfunction is naturally suspected as the cause of the fatal accident. An aeronautical and a mechanical engineer specializing in such matters are retained, and their studies indicate that the plane's engine showed no signs of operation upon impact. They surmise that the fuel system was defective and that the pilot shut down the engine shortly after he lost power.

Scenario 2: A Pennsylvania oil and gas company has been sued for draining valuable reserves off a tract of adjoining land, and potentially millions of dollars are at stake. A petroleum engineer is hired to conduct extensive seismic studies, and they reveal that no drainage occurred.

Scenario 3: Several young associates in a Wall Street law firm are handling a case that involves the production of at least ten million documents. The client, a large multinational corporation, has failed to adequately organize its files, and some technical expertise is needed to render the mounds of paperwork electronically retrievable.

Scenario 4: A small auto-parts store is forced to go out of business because the distributor supplying it has breached numerous contractual provisions regarding special allowances. The company needs an accounting expert who can prepare profit-margin comparisons between the retailer and the competition to see if an antitrust suit is in order.

Scenario 5: Though she is wearing expensive eyeguards, a proficient racquetball player, suffers serious injury when a furious cross-court volley hits her in the left eye. An expert will testify that the eyeguard failed to protect her as claimed in the company's extensive advertising campaign. The company does not believe that the plaintiff's expert is qualified and plans to object strenuously to the admission of the expert's opinion.

These and a thousand similar scenarios are the routine plight of the litigator, and they involve that one common and challenging denominator—finding a credible expert witness. In today's litigation scene, retaining top-notch experts—those who are well qualified and who, after tenaciously examining the facts of your case, will acquire the specialized knowledge to present it—is more important than ever. Complicated factual issues make it imperative that your experts be effective communicators capable of both educating you and the client before trial, and persuading the judge and jury at trial.

As the world becomes increasingly sophisticated, jurors are more skeptical than ever of experts who will take whichever position earns them a healthy fee. Judicial fact finders now have to be strongly convinced of the truth of your position.

The Decision to Retain an Expert

The first consideration is whether an expert should even be retained. In some cases it may not be necessary, or even wise, to hire an expert. For example, in those situations where a layperson could competently provide the same testimony, an expert should not be used. The court would undoubtedly disallow such testimony in any event and therefore leave the jury to their own understanding.

Some aspects of a case may be proven without the need of an expert even if the information is not readily apparent to the jury. For instance, laypeople can in many instances testify to the market value of real property as long as those matters are within their personal knowledge.

And there may be instances where an expert would overly complicate the case, or where the jury would find an expert intimidating or intrusive. Common sense and good judgment about whether to hire an expert should be your guide in each of these instances.

Role of the Expert Witness

In many cases, an expert witness is an absolute necessity in order to legally establish a claim or a defense. Without an expert, the claim or defense will be swiftly dismissed. In other cases, the expert may not be legally required, but will serve as an indispensable force of persuasion.

How you as a lawyer utilize an expert witness naturally depends to a large extent upon the particular facts of the case before you. That said, the uses of experts in modern-day litigation are myriad, as discussed in the following sections.

Assessing the Case

The advantages of retaining an effective expert for presentation of a case at trial are well known, but an expert can also prove helpful in the very early stages of litigation. If you have not yet committed yourself to accept the case—or you are willing to take it on but your client has not yet decided to bring suit—an expert may be extremely useful in assessing the viability of the case.

The expert can, for example, suggest vital areas of inquiry that you should undertake with the client and perhaps other individuals. The expert may also be helpful in locating and reviewing relevant documents that shed further light on the nature of the situation before you.

An expert can also be helpful in evaluating the strength of the opponent's claims. The ability of an expert to point out inconsistencies in the opposing party's position, and to make further suggestions for attacking them, is often invaluable. Sometimes, by the very selection of a respected expert that the opposing party recognizes and respects, you may well undermine their case.

Discovering Facts

An expert can dramatically improve the substance of discovery in both propounding and answering interrogatories, requests for admissions, and document requests. Where the opposition has given you a list of potential witnesses, the expert can frequently help select the best individuals for you to depose. The expert may also prove effective in gathering further information about these experts' qualifications, experience, and prior testimony.

If the case involves a large number of documents or a complicated records system, an expert can set up programs where data received from both the client and the adversary can be stored and easily retrieved. It may also be that only an expert can tell what should have been produced by the other side but appears to be missing.

The expert can also assist you in responding to requests for documents. No self-respecting lawyer would think of turning over documents without knowing what they contain and how they may affect the case at a later stage. If the expert identifies extremely damaging documents, it may be time to make a settlement offer before the case deteriorates.

Drafting Documents

When you are preparing to draft the necessary motions and other legal documents required in litigation, an expert can be helpful in shaping legal theories and in identifying the many pitfalls inherent in the field. The expert can also ensure that the appropriate nomenclature is used.

Cornerstone of Expert Testimony

The cornerstone of expert testimony is Federal Rule of Evidence 702, which has been widely emulated in the state courts. It provides that a qualified expert may offer an opinion that is based on sufficient facts or data and is the product of reliable principles and methods that have been reliably applied to the facts of the case.

Taking Depositions

The expert can help you prepare for, take, and defend depositions. You should not depose the other side's expert without having your own expert present. Even the deposition of fact witnesses will be more thorough if you are assisted by an expert.

The expert can also help you prepare your own witnesses for deposition. With your expert's knowledge and healthy skepticism in the preparation of witnesses, vulnerable areas can be probed and challenging questions anticipated. Aware of these problems in advance, your witness will be better prepared and more relaxed in the deposition.

Planning for Trial

An expert can of course be essential in planning for trial. The expert may, for instance, provide guidance as to the clearest and most dramatic way to present evidence as exhibits. An expert can alert you to the need for other experts at trial and make useful suggestions. And the expert can be of assistance in preparing for cross-examination of your experts and those of the opposing side.

Trying the Case

The expert's role in helping the trier of fact understand the evidence and determine factual issues is well appreciated. An impressive expert lends immeasurable credibility to your client's case. Cases are often won or lost simply on the strength of expert testimony.

In complicated cases where your party is an underdog and faces a formidable burden, you will inevitably lose if your expert cannot help the jury understand the case. The instructional skills and courtroom performance of an adept and experienced expert can give you the critical edge needed to overcome the formidable odds at trial.

Consulting and Testifying Experts

For purposes of litigation, and particularly discovery matters, experts are typically separated into two broad camps—those expected to testify at trial and those who are not. When an expert plans to testify, opposing parties are allowed substantial scrutiny, and they may legitimately inquire into the expert's background, the subject matters on which the expert will testify, and the substance of the opinions expressed. Obtaining discovery from nontestifying, or consulting, experts is much more difficult. A party wishing to obtain discovery of these experts must plead exceptional circumstances showing that obtaining facts or opinions by other means would be impractical, a difficult burden to meet.

Expert Qualifications

The initial issue is an obvious one: Is the potential expert qualified to give testimony in the case at hand? In federal courts and most state courts, evidentiary rules provide that expert opinion testimony may be given by any witness who has the "scientific, technical, or other specialized knowledge" to assist the trier of fact in "understanding the evidence or determining a fact in issue." Therefore, the basic threshold questions of an expert's qualifications become: (1) does the witness possess the requisite scientific, technical, or other specialized knowledge, and (2) will that knowledge be helpful to the judge and jury?

The evidentiary rules regarding experts have been increasingly liberalized over the years, and these standards are intended to be broadly inclusive, permitting expert testimony on a wide range of topics. Experts may be drawn from almost any field of endeavor as long as they can be shown to possess this specialized knowledge, which need not necessarily result from formal education but which in appropriate circumstances may be based exclusively on practical experience.

▼▼▼▼▼

Expert Challenges

An expert can expect to be challenged by the other party on such issues as

◆ Qualifications

◆ Knowledge of the case

◆ Bias or interest in the case

◆ Conflicting expert opinions or previous testimony

◆ Fees for services rendered

Admissibility of Testimony

In most jurisdictions, the judge must make a preliminary assessment of the validity, reasoning, and methodology of an expert's opinion before that information is presented to the fact finder. The judge in essence acts as a gatekeeper, deciding whether the proposed testimony is reliable enough to be presented to the fact finder.

Under this approach, the judge must initially determine whether an expert's methodology and conclusions are of sufficient substance to qualify as evidence, or whether they should instead be dismissed as "junk science." If the opinion of an expert witness is challenged by the other party, the judge typically holds a hearing to determine whether the expert should be allowed to proceed.

Under the older and now largely abandoned *Frye* rule, scientific testimony was admissible *only* if the witness's test and procedures had gained general acceptance within the relevant scientific or technical community. Under this approach, innovative procedures could not form the basis of expert testimony until they had been adopted, or at least recognized, by a broader scientific audience.

This qualification required prominent substantiation such as publication in a peer-reviewed journal. This is no longer the case under the federal rules.

▼▼▼▼▼

Effective Expert Testimony

The value of an effective expert can hardly be overstated, as illustrated by this brief exchange on direct examination:

Q: Could you tell us what the tests show us about any evidence of a heart attack in this case?

A: As I have summarized, a heart attack can be diagnosed by two different means—clinical and pathological. So let's go through them one by one.

   Were there symptoms of a heart attack—history of chest pain, left arm pain, numbness in the chin? From my reading of Mrs. Durrett's deposition, there was no type of specific symptom which would suggest a myocardial infarction. So I think we can cross that out.

   Were there EKG findings of a myocardial infarction? There were not. But, in fairness, the patient was already in ventricular fibrillation, so we didn't really have a rhythm which could have shown ST segment depression or ST segment elevation or T-wave inversions or a Q wave—some of the EKG findings of a heart attack. So it's really noninformative. So, I'm only going to put one "X" through that. We don't have evidence of it, but we don't have all the material that we would have liked to have had to be able to completely say that the EKG did not show a MI.

   What about the enzymes? These were not drawn, so we have no evidence of enzymes in the blood to indicate there was a heart attack. But since we don't know either way, I'm not going to put an "X;" I'm going to put one line through it.

   What about pathology? Where there any gross changes to the naked eye? There were none. So I'm going to put an "X" on that one.

   Was there microscopic evidence? The first microscopic evidence should appear six hours after a myocardial infarction. But there wasn't any. There was no evidence that the

> heart muscle was dead before the patient died completely. So I'm going to put an "X" there.
>
> Finally, was there a thrombus like the one I showed you in the photograph? Not only was there no evidence of a clot, but there was no sign of a fissured plaque. So I can put an "X" there.

Helpfulness to the Fact Finder

If the expert's opinion "will assist the trier of fact to understand the evidence or to determine a fact in issue," as Federal Rule of Evidence 702 phrases it, the proponent is beyond the first hurdle. Even when jurors are capable of deciding a matter based on their own experience, an expert may still have specialized knowledge that will prove helpful.

The Opinion's Basis

Under the older rules, an expert had to spend a great deal of time first establishing the basis of the opinion. But under the federal rules, the expert can rely on evidence that consists of inadmissible hearsay or violates other exclusionary rules, as long as the evidence is reasonably relied upon by experts in that particular field.

The Opinion's Scope

It was once considered improper for an expert to offer an opinion on the "ultimate issue" in the case, since this was regarded as improperly invading the province of the jury. This restrictive rule often led to extremely elliptical testimony, with the expert testifying to a series of inferences and opinions but never quite reaching the most obvious factual conclusions. The process was further complicated by the difficulty of determining exactly which issues were ultimate and which ones were not.

The federal rules now provide that expert testimony, if otherwise admissible, is not objectionable simply because it embraces the ultimate issue. An important exception is that an expert in a criminal case may not provide an opinion on whether the defendant had the mental state or condition constituting an element of the crime charged or its defense.

Revealing the Opinion's Foundation

Under current federal rules (and those of many states), an expert can offer an opinion with or without first explaining the facts or data on which the opinion is based. In theory, an expert can simply state his or her opinion on direct examination. In practice, however, this approach is rarely, if ever, followed, since an expert's opinion can hardly be persuasive until its underlying foundation is explained. The practical effect of Federal Rule of Evidence 703, which governs the bases of expert opinion testimony, is to allow the witness to first state the opinion and then follow it up by an explanation, rather than having to tediously set forth all the expert's biographical data in the beginning.

Rule 703 contemplates that the underlying foundation for the expert's opinion will be elicited on cross-examination, especially given that the federal rules permit extensive discovery of an expert's opinions and the bases for those opinions.

Disclosure of Witness Materials

The complexity and importance of expert testimony has placed a renewed emphasis on the importance of discovery. A lawyer cannot effectively cross-examine the other party's expert without adequate preparation and knowledge of the expert's opinions.

Practically everything that expert witnesses review is discoverable if it forms part of their opinions. Naturally, this provides a potential minefield of problems for parties presenting experts, since they invariably wish to keep some matters, such as attorney work-product, confidential.

Some courts hold that all such materials reviewed by the expert are discoverable, regardless of whether the information is factual or whether it contains counsel's mental impressions. Other courts hold that only the factual portions of communications are discoverable in order to protect counsel's core work-product.

Expert Compensation

Under federal rules, the court may require a party seeking discovery from the opposing party's testifying expert to pay a reasonable fee for time spent in responding to discovery. For depositions, the party seeking discovery ordinarily will pay the expert's fee for the time spent preparing for the deposition, traveling to be deposed, attending the deposition, and returning from the deposition.

In evaluating whether a proposed expert fee is reasonable, courts have considered such factors as the area of expertise; the education and training required; the prevailing rates; the nature, quality, and complexity of the discovery responses; the cost of living in the area; the fee being charged by the expert to the retaining party; and fees traditionally charged by the expert on similar matters.

Standard of Review

When reviewing allegedly improper testimony objected to at trial, appellate courts must determine whether the error had a substantial or injurious effect or influence in determining the jury's verdict, and they will evaluate the severity of the error and the trial record as a whole. In matters related to expert witnesses, appellate courts typically apply an abuse of discretion review and will reverse the trial court only on a clear showing of abuse and "substantial influence" on the jury's verdict.

The Legal Framework

2

EXPERT TESTIMONY, HAVING BECOME such an integral part of the litigation scene, has been increasingly scrutinized by the legislatures and the courts. The common law at first struggled with the very idea of such testimony, fearful of the undue influence of overly persuasive experts on the minds of the jury. Even as evidentiary rules developed, there was always skepticism toward the testimony of experts.

In 1923 the *Frye* case articulated a "general acceptance" test in which expert testimony was allowed if it was generally accepted within the relevant expert community. That test remained the law for 70 years until the Supreme Court issued the *Daubert* opinion in 1993.

The following brief history of the legal framework regarding expert witnesses should help you in developing—and attacking—expert testimony in the cases you handle.

Common Law

Before procedural or evidentiary rules were adopted, the courts themselves had to determine when witnesses could testify beyond that which they had personally observed. In the case of lay witnesses, the courts tended to restrict testimony to facts within the witness's personal knowledge. However, the line between fact and opinion was often difficult to draw, and if the opinion was a shorthand rendition of fact, it was usually admitted.

Witnesses were prohibited from giving an ultimate opinion because that was considered to be an inference that the jury was capable of making. Courts were concerned that juries might be unduly swayed by witnesses whose opinions were highly regarded.

The courts, however, soon recognized that some subjects were beyond the understanding of jurors, who needed useful assistance to resolve these issues. The courts also realized that it was not always possible to supply the jury with sufficient information to allow them to draw their own conclusions. In these circumstances, they permitted expert witnesses to testify, leaving the jury to determine the weight and credibility to be given the testimony.

The common law recognized only two permissible bases for expert opinions: firsthand knowledge (such as that of a treating physician) and facts presented at trial through the testimony of other witnesses or in answer to a properly formulated hypothetical question. In both cases, the facts were clearly identifiable.

Early Evidence Rules

Traditionally, there was a strong skepticism with regard to expert testimonial evidence. At early common law, the courts did not permit such evidence for fear that a witness would be biased toward one of the parties. Over time this skepticism dissipated as the courts created institutional safeguards to ensure competent witnesses and developed more formal rules governing the admissibility of expert testimony. The expert could be utilized only if the testimony would be helpful in understanding the facts of the case. The opinion of an expert witness, if not based on personal observation, had to be grounded on facts established by evidence admitted at trial. If the facts upon which the expert based the opinion were not within the expert's firsthand knowledge, the opinion had to be given in response to a hypothetical question.

As confidence in the adversarial system and its evidentiary standards increased, the issue became one of how the court could independently evaluate the expertise claimed by the witness or the conclusions the expert had reached. The courts debated whether it was proper for the court to screen out testimony based on no more than speculation or belief of a purported expert, or whether the jury should be permitted to hear the evidence without judicial interference. The Supreme Court addressed this question in *Frye.*

The Frye Test

Until the early twentieth century, the courts evaluated the admissibility of expert testimony by the traditional relevancy standard. Not until 1923, with the articulation of the "general acceptance" test in the case of *Frye v. United States,* 293 F. 1013 (D.C. Cir. 1923), did the courts recognize the notion of a special rule for admissibility of scientific evidence. This standard required that scientific expert testimony be not only relevant but also sufficiently established to have gained general acceptance in the particular field.

In *Frye,* the trial court refused to admit testimony of the criminal defendant's expert, who wanted to testify about the results of a "systolic blood-pressure deception test." The defendant claimed that the test accurately revealed whether the subject was lying by recording changes in systolic blood pressure. (The defendant had obviously done well on the test.) The court, however, sustained the prosecutor's objection to admission of the test. When the jury convicted the defendant of murder, he appealed.

The appellate court affirmed Frye's conviction. Although earlier cases had allowed opinion testimony of witnesses skilled in a particular science, art, or trade, the court explained that not all such opinions were admissible:

> Just when a scientific principle or discovery crosses the line between the experimental and demonstrable stages is difficult to define. Somewhere in this twilight zone the evidential force of the principle must be recognized, and while courts will go a long way in admitting expert testimony deduced from a well-recognized scientific principle or discovery, the thing from which the deduction is made must be sufficiently established to have gained general acceptance in the particular field in which it belongs.

The court therefore sustained the trial court's decision to exclude the test results. For the next 70 years the courts used this general acceptance test to evaluate expert testimony.

Beginnings of Change

One advantage of the *Frye* test was that it relieved courts of the responsibility of independently determining the reliability of scientific evidence. This in turn reduced the time and attention necessary to issue these rulings, and it permitted the court to leave the ultimate determination to the scientific community, where many felt the decision belonged anyway.

Many legal commentators complained of the opinion's disadvantages. The rule tended to be inflexible; new scientific knowledge that was both relevant and reliable was rendered inadmissible if the scientific community had not yet widely accepted it. The courts also struggled with such issues as how to define the relevant scientific community, what the term "general acceptance" included, whether the standard applied to both "the underlying principle and the technique applying it," and whether to apply the test only to novel scientific evidence or to all scientific evidence. The *Frye* test stood dominant for decades and the debate raged on.

In the latter half of the twentieth century, a number of courts decided to restrict or altogether reject the *Frye* test. As a result, admissibility of expert testimony in some of these jurisdictions became extremely lenient, allowing almost anyone who claimed specialized knowledge to testify. As use of expert witnesses expanded, there was concern about the admission of opinions based on pseudoscience, or what was commonly referred to as "junk science."

▼▼▼▼▼

Daubert on General Acceptance

"To summarize: 'General acceptance' is not a necessary precondition to the admissibility of scientific evidence under the Federal Rules of Evidence, but the Rules of Evidence—especially Rule 702—do assign to the trial judge the task of ensuring that an expert's testimony both rests on a reliable foundation and is relevant to the task at hand."

Daubert, 509 U.S. at 597.

1975 Federal Rules of Evidence

To meet growing concerns about the credibility of expert testimony, Congress enacted in 1975 a new set of federal evidentiary rules, which included the first version of the now pivotal Rule 702:

> If scientific, technical, or other specialized knowledge will assist the trier of fact to understand the evidence or to determine a fact in issue, a witness qualified as an expert by knowledge, skill, experience, training, or education, may testify thereto in the form of an opinion or otherwise.

It was especially notable that Rule 702 did not contain the requirement that the expert's opinion be "generally accepted" as required by the *Frye* decision.

Other federal evidentiary rules were enacted in 1975 as well. Rule 703 broadened the permissible bases of expert opinion to include any evidence, admissible or not, as long as experts in the field would reasonably rely upon that basis. Rule 704 abolished the rule prohibiting experts from testifying on ultimate issues, which until then was believed to be the province of the jury. And Rule 705 abandoned the requirement that an expert first disclose facts underlying the opinion as a prerequisite to admissibility of the opinion itself.

Continued Application of Frye

The conflict among the courts over application of the *Frye* opinion after enactment of Rule 702 indicated the general confusion and growing disapproval of the test. In fact, the drafting history of Rule 702 did not even mention *Frye*. The Federal Rules of Evidence as a whole sought to adopt a more liberal approach toward admission of relevant evidence, leading many commentators to conclude that *Frye* did not survive the adoption of the new rules.

Some courts therefore held that the new rules superseded *Frye,* while others manipulated the test or rejected it for other reasons and began using a reliability standard. For example, the Second Circuit in *United States v. Williams,* 583 F.2d 1194 (1978), declined to follow the *Frye* standard and instead attempted to determine reliability through the application of several factors. The court noted specifically that a determination of reliability could not rest solely on a process of "counting scientific noses." The court articulated several factors that indicated reliability, and these included the potential rate of error, the existence and maintenance of standards, the care taken with the methodology, and similarity with other scientific techniques. *Williams* concluded that Rule 702 had superseded the *Frye* test and created a more liberal approach to the admission of scientific expert testimony.

Similarly, the Third Circuit in *United States v. Downing,* 753 F.2d 1224 (1985), rejected the *Frye* test primarily because of policy considerations, noting that *Frye* relied upon vague terms that allowed courts to manipulate the parameters of the relevant scientific community and the level of agreement needed for general acceptance. The court pointed out that novel but reliable scientific techniques were often excluded under *Frye* and therefore unnecessarily impeded truth-seeking.

For years the circuit courts remained divided over the applicability of *Frye*. While a majority of courts still followed the general acceptance standard, a growing number rejected it. The conflict among the circuits and the confusion in the application of *Frye* and Rule 702 remained unresolved until 1993—18 years later—when the Supreme Court decided the *Daubert* case.

Courts as Gatekeepers

As a result of Federal Rule of Evidence 702, the *Daubert* case, and other decisions following, the courts, in an attempt to screen out unreliable expert testimony, become obliged to act as gatekeepers.

Daubert: *Admission of Scientific Evidence*

A watershed moment in the field of expert scientific testimony occurred when the Supreme Court decided in *Daubert v. Merrell Dow Pharmaceuticals, Inc.,* 509 U.S. 579 (1993), that Rule 702 superseded the 70-year-old *Frye* test. (See Chapter 3 for a detailed discussion of the *Daubert* case.)

The plaintiffs in *Daubert* sought compensation from manufacturers of the drug Bendectin for birth defects allegedly caused by the drug. The district court granted summary judgment to the defendants because the methodology of plaintiffs' causation experts was not generally accepted under the *Frye* test. The Ninth Circuit affirmed the summary judgment.

Vacating those decisions, the Supreme Court held that the new and more liberal rules of evidence had rendered null and void the strict *Frye* test. The Court interpreted Rule 702 as requiring the trial court to ensure that "any and all scientific testimony or evidence admitted is not only relevant, but reliable," and that it should do this by conducting a two-step inquiry.

Daubert held, first of all, that the trial court must assess whether the reasoning of the proposed expert testimony is scientifically valid. This requires the court to weigh what are now known as the *Daubert* factors: (1) whether the reasoning is testable, (2) whether the reasoning has undergone peer review, (3) the error rate of the technique used, and (4) whether the reasoning has been generally accepted in its relevant discipline. Secondly, *Daubert* held that the trial court must assess whether the proposed scientific testimony would assist the fact finder in determining a fact at issue. Once an expert has met these requirements by a preponderance of the evidence, the expert's testimony will be deemed admissible.

Although *Daubert* was beneficial in that it provided trial judges with a tool for determining reliable and relevant scientific evidence, it still left several questions unanswered: (1) whether the *Daubert* factors applied to all expert evidence or only scientific evidence, (2) whether the application of the *Daubert* factors was required or merely suggested, and (3) whether the decision to apply the factors was subject to an abuse-of-discretion standard or to a de novo review. The ambiguous language of the *Daubert* decision required federal courts to wrestle with the answers to these questions for years to come.

▼▼▼▼▼

The Applicability of *Daubert*

"The conclusion, in our view, is that we can neither rule out, nor rule in, for all cases and for all time the applicability of the factors mentioned in *Daubert*, nor can we now do so for subsets of cases categorized by category of expert or by kind of evidence. Too much depends upon the particular circumstances of the particular case at issue."

Kumho Tire, 526 U.S. at 151

Kumho Tire: *Admission of Nonscientific Evidence*

In *Kumho Tire Co., Ltd. v. Carmichael,* 526 U.S. 137 (1999), the Supreme Court finally put to rest the contradictory applications of *Daubert* by extending the trial judge's gatekeeping function to nonscientific expert evidence as well. (See Chapter 3 for a detailed discussion of the *Kumho Tire* case.)

The Court in *Kumho Tire* stated that a trial judge must serve as a gatekeeper to *all* expert evidence, and that the judge may apply the *Daubert* factors to nonscientific evidence.

The Court also asserted that the application of the *Daubert* factors was not a requisite formality for admitting or excluding evidence, and that the trial judge could consider any appropriate factors when evaluating the evidence. In other words, the *Daubert* factors were not a definitive checklist to determine admissibility, but factors that could be used if helpful.

Kumho Tire nevertheless provided a clear mandate to trial courts: When the testimony of an expert is called into question, the trial judge must determine whether the testimony has a reliable basis in the knowledge and experience of the relevant discipline.

Revised Rule 702

Federal Rule of Evidence 702 governs the admission of expert testimony and requires that experts first establish that their testimony will assist the fact finder's understanding of the evidence. (See Chapter 5 for further discussion of the federal evidentiary rules.)

Rule 702 does not require that the subject matter be complex—it requires only that the expert's testimony assist the jury. (The court must first make a preliminary determination under Rule 104(a) that the witness is qualified to give an expert opinion.) Pursuant to Rule 702, a witness may qualify as an expert by knowledge, skill, experience, training, or education. Thus, anyone with specialized knowledge may qualify as an expert in a particular area.

The clear language of Rule 702 applies to *all* expert testimony. The language of the rule does not distinguish between "scientific," "technical," or "other specialized" knowledge. The Court in *Daubert* stated that the "gatekeeping" function was derived from the word "knowledge," not the words that modify it. Rule 702 states that "scientific" is not the only word that modifies "knowledge." The legislative history of the rule also supports a broad application of Rule 702 to all types of experts.

Since its enactment, Rule 702 has allowed experts to testify when their "scientific, technical, or other specialized knowledge will assist the trier of fact to understand the evidence or to determine a fact in issue." For almost 20 years, however, federal trial courts struggled to interpret Rule 702 because it did not explain how to evaluate expert testimony. The Supreme Court, in both the *Daubert* and *Kumho Tire* decisions, finally explained how federal courts should apply the rule.

As a result, Rule 702 was changed in 2000 and was similar but with an important addition (shown in italics):

> If scientific, technical, or other specialized knowledge will assist the trier of fact to understand the evidence or to determine a fact in issue, a witness qualified as an expert by knowledge, skill, experience, training, or education, may testify thereto in the form of an opinion or otherwise, *if (1) the testimony is based upon sufficient facts or data, (2) the testimony is the product of reliable principles and methods, and (3) the witness has applied the principles and methods reliably to the facts of the case.*

Consistent with the Court's conclusions in *Kumho Tire,* the rule does not establish separate tests for expert testimony based on scientific and nonscientific knowledge. Subpart (1) ensures that experts have adequate reason for reaching the conclusion about which they propose to testify. Subpart (2) examines how the expert reached his or her conclusion from the facts or data scrutinized. Even if the expert has adequate knowledge or experience in the subject of the testimony, the expert must also employ reasonable processes to reach a conclusion. And Subpart (3) requires that the expert's conclusions themselves are a reasonable result of the process and supporting facts.

Rule 702 therefore provides general guidance to trial judges about how to apply the factors of reliability. By focusing a trial judge's attention on three aspects of an expert's testimony, the rule provides criteria sufficiently general to address any type of expert testimony.

▼▼▼▼▼

Abuse of Discretion

"The trial court must have the same kind of latitude in deciding *how* to test an expert's reliability, and to decide whether or when special briefing or other proceedings are needed to investigate reliability, as it enjoys when it decides *whether or not* that expert's relevant testimony is reliable. Our opinion in *Joiner* makes clear that a court of appeals is to apply an abuse-of-discretion standard when it 'review[s] a trial court's decision to admit or exclude expert testimony.'"

Kumho Tire, 526 U.S. at 152

Other Evidentiary Rules

Other evidentiary rules also promulgated the increasing liberalization of expert witness testimony. Federal Rule of Evidence 703 dramatically expanded the permissible basis for expert testimony. Prior to its enactment, an expert witness could rely only on facts or data that had been personally observed or made known to the witness at or before trial. An expert may still rely on either of those bases to form an opinion, but Rule 703 provided an additional third basis (shown in italics) on which an expert may rely:

> The facts or data in the particular case upon which an expert bases an opinion or inference may be those perceived by or made known to him at or before the hearing. *If of a type reasonably relied upon by experts in the particular field in forming opinions or inferences upon the subject, the facts or data need not be admissible in evidence in order for the opinion or inference to be admitted.*

Likewise, Federal Rule of Evidence 705 abandoned the requirement that an expert disclose facts underlying the opinion as a prerequisite to admissibility of the opinion itself. The rule instead contemplates that the underlying foundation for the expert's opinion will be elicited on cross-examination.

And Federal Rule of Evidence 704 eliminated the prohibition on the ability of an expert to express an opinion on the ultimate issue in a case, which was formerly considered the exclusive domain of the jury.

Discovery of Experts

The materials that a party requests of an opposing expert are the subject of numerous procedural rules and court cases. (See Chapter 4 for a further discussion of expert discovery.)

The area is full of traps for the unwary, often requiring discovery of any materials even remotely considered by the expert in arriving at an opinion. Attorneys must be especially careful when retaining experts who have been contacted by the opposing party, in order to prevent disqualification of the expert or, worse, of the attorney.

The complexity and importance of cases requiring extensive expert testimony have placed a renewed emphasis on the importance of discovery. It is also duly noted that an attorney cannot effectively cross-examine the other party's expert without adequate preparation and knowledge of that expert's opinions.

The Federal Rules of Civil Procedure outline in some detail the discovery parameters of expert witnesses who are expected to testify at trial. The rules provide, among other things, that a party may submit interrogatories and take depositions concerning the subject matter on which the expert is expected to testify, the substance of the facts and opinions to be asserted by the expert, and the underlying grounds for each opinion. The court may of course order additional discovery and otherwise regulate the timing, scope, and nature of discovery.

Attorney-Client Privilege

Although the federal rules require the disclosure of information considered by expert witnesses in forming their opinions, the rules do protect from discovery the lawyer's work-product by excluding "mental impressions, conclusions, opinions, or legal theories of an attorney." Thus, communications between counsel and expert that incorporate the lawyer's core work-product are traditionally not discoverable, while those that form the basis of the expert's opinion may be.

The courts have taken inconsistent approaches when applying the discovery rules to communications that incorporate this core work-product. The growing trend is to permit thorough discovery, including communications that would otherwise be privileged. Other courts compel discovery but protect core work-product by redacting the privileged sections.

The ambiguities of the rules provide little reassurance for lawyers trying to protect against unwarranted disclosure. This is more cumbersome and time-consuming, but there are grave consequences for failure to do so.

Appropriate Standard of Review

What standard will the appellate court apply to decisions regarding expert witnesses? In *General Electric Co. v. Joiner,* 522 U.S. 136 (1997), the Supreme Court resolved another question left unanswered by *Daubert*—the correct standard of review applicable to the trial court's evidentiary rulings. Reaffirming its prior holdings, the Court held that the proper standard of review pertaining to a trial court's evidentiary rulings on expert witnesses is the abuse of discretion standard.

The Court additionally addressed the argument that *Daubert* focused solely on principles and methodology, not conclusions. The Court held that conclusions and methodology are not entirely distinct from each other, and thus the abuse-of-discretion review is not confined solely to the methodologies of the expert but also includes the expert's conclusions.

▼▼▼▼▼

Evaluating Reliability

Some of the factors a court may consider when evaluating the reliability of an expert's theory or technique:

♦ Whether it has been tested.

♦ The rate of error.

♦ Whether it has undergone peer review and publication.

- ◆ General acceptance within the relevant scientific community.

- ◆ Whether the theory or technique was developed solely for litigation.

- ◆ Whether alternative explanations have been eliminated.

Supreme Court Decisions 3

W<small>HEN IT COMES TO</small> expert witness, the two most prominent Supreme Court cases are *Daubert* and *Kumho Tire,* and the practitioner seeking to introduce or to prevent expert testimony is well advised to become intimately familiar with each. (See Appendices for the texts of the decisions.)

The present law of expert witness testimony was in a state of flux only a dozen or so years ago. Federal Rule of Evidence 702 had been enacted in 1975, but into the early 1990s the courts were unsure whether the old "general acceptance" test still applied. *Daubert* settled that issue in favor of the federal rule. But the question remained whether it applied only to scientific evidence. *Kumho Tire* resolved that question in favor of expanding the gatekeeping function to all cases and without the rigidity of the four factors of reliability enumerated in *Daubert.* Both cases sought to ensure that all expert testimony is both relevant *and* reliable.

The *Daubert* Opinion

In *Daubert v. Merrell Dow Pharmaceuticals, Inc.,* 509 U.S. 579 (1993), two couples, acting on behalf of their sons who were deformed at birth, sued Merrell Dow Pharmaceuticals, the manufacturer of the antinausea drug Bendectin. The families alleged that their sons' birth defects had been caused by the mothers' ingestion of Bendectin during pregnancy.

Dow moved for summary judgment because no scientific evidence linked Bendectin to human birth defects. Dow produced an expert who had reviewed all the literature on Bendectin and human birth defects, and he testified that no study had found the drug to be a human teratogen.

The plaintiffs opposed Dow's motion for summary judgment by producing testimony from eight experts. These experts asserted that a study of Bendectin-related birth defects in animals showed a similarity of the chemical composition of Bendectin and other known teratogens, and that a synthesis of existing epidemiological studies showed that Bendectin could cause human birth defects. The court noted that the expert analysis of plaintiffs was neither published nor reviewed by other scientists. Invoking *Frye*'s general acceptance test, the district court granted Dow's motion for summary judgment.

On appeal, the Ninth Circuit Court of Appeals applied the *Frye* test and affirmed the summary judgment. Like the district court, the Ninth Circuit highlighted the fact that the analysis was "not subjected to the normal peer review process and was generated solely for use in litigation."

Issues Presented

The Supreme Court granted plaintiff's petition for certiorari to consider two questions: (1) whether *Frye* remained valid law after enactment of the Federal Rules of Evidence, and (2) if so, whether the case required expert scientific testimony to be subjected to a peer review process in order to be admissible. In reversing the summary judgment, the Court agreed that Federal Rule of Evidence 702, not the *Frye* test, was the prevailing standard for expert testimony.

Noting that nothing in Rule 702 established general acceptance as a prerequisite to admissibility, the Court concluded that the *Frye* test was effectively displaced by the federal rules. However, the Court emphasized that this did not mean the trial judge was unable to screen scientific evidence. To the contrary, under the federal evidentiary rules the trial judge *must* ensure that all scientific testimony is not only relevant but reliable. Therefore, to aid trial judges in reviewing expert testimony, the Court offered four factors.

The Four Factors

The four reliability factors offered by the Court, although neither exclusive nor mandatory, were (1) whether the scientific technique or theory can (and has been) tested; (2) whether the theory or technique has been subjected to peer review and publication; (3) the theory's known or potential rate of error and the existence and maintenance of standards controlling the technique's operation; and, (4) confirming that *Frye* was displaced as the prevailing standard, whether the reasoning has been generally accepted in its relevant discipline. Equipped with these guidelines, trial court judges must assume a gatekeeping role of ensuring that an expert's testimony both rests on a reliable foundation and is relevant to the case at hand.

Applicability to Non-Scientific Evidence

In his partial concurrence, Chief Justice Rehnquist raised the issue that was later presented in *Kumho Tire* (discussed below). The Chief Justice asked whether the Court's four factors applied to an expert seeking to testify on the basis of "technical or other specialized knowledge"—the other types of expert knowledge to which Rule 702 applies—or only to scientific knowledge.

Responses of Circuit Courts

The Court in *Daubert* seemed to limit its holding to scientific expert testimony. As a result, the circuit courts applying *Daubert* did not take a uniform approach—some courts limited its application to scientific testimony, while others applied the standard to technical and other types of testimony.

For example, the Seventh Circuit, in *Cummins v. Lyle Industries,* 93 F. 3d 362 (1996), held that the *Daubert* factors *did* apply to expert testimony other than scientific. The court examined the language from *Daubert* and noted that while the holding was limited to scientific expert testimony, the Supreme Court did state that its holding was not limited to cases involving "novel" scientific theories. The court concluded that the task of the district court remained essentially the same—to ensure that the testimony is of an acceptable level of reliability.

On the other hand, the Tenth Circuit, in *Compton v. Subaru of America, Inc.,* 82 F.3d 1513 (1996), concluded that the *Daubert* analysis did *not* apply to the admissibility of all kinds of expert testimony. The court recognized the gatekeeping duty of *Daubert,* but concluded that the *Daubert* factors were not applicable to cases where the expert testimony was based solely on experience or training.

With no guidance from the Supreme Court on this question of nonscientific experts, an inevitable split among the circuits arose. Two circuits—the Fifth and Sixth—held that *Daubert* and its four-part test of scientific validity applied to all expert testimony. The First, Third, Seventh, and Eighth Circuits held that the reliability requirement *Daubert* required for scientific testimony should apply to nonscientific evidence, but that the trial judge need not apply the four-part test. The other circuits—the Second, Fourth, Ninth, Tenth, and Eleventh—held that *Daubert* applied only to scientific evidence. The Supreme Court, recognizing the diverse approaches, granted certiorari in *Kumho Tire* to address the effect of *Daubert* on nonscientific expert testimony.

▼▼▼▼▼

The Flexibility of *Daubert*

"The inquiry envisioned by Rule 702 is, we emphasize, a flexible one. Its overarching subject is the scientific validity—and thus the evidentiary relevance and reliability—of the principles that underlie a proposed submission. The focus, of course, must be solely on principles and methodology, not on the conclusions they generate.

"Throughout, a judge assessing a proffer of expert scientific testimony under Rule 702 should also be mindful of other applicable rules. Rule 703 provides that expert opinions based on otherwise inadmissible hearsay are to be admitted only if the facts or data are 'of a type reasonably relied upon by experts in the particular field in forming opinions or influences upon the subject.' Rule 706 allows the court at its discretion to procure the assistance of an expert of its own choosing. Finally, Rule 403 permits the exclusion of relevant evidence 'if its probative value is substantially outweighed by the danger of unfair prejudice, confusion of the issues, or misleading the jury. . . .'"

Daubert, 509 U.S. at 594–95.

The *Kumho Tire* Opinion

The plaintiffs in *Kumho Tire Co., Ltd. v. Carmichael,* 526 U.S. 137 (1999), were injured in a single-vehicle accident in Baldwin County, Alabama. The accident occurred when the driver lost control after his right rear tire blew out. The vehicle overturned, ejecting six of its eight occupants.

Plaintiffs brought suit against the tire manufacturer, claiming that the tire was defective. Plaintiffs' tire-failure expert testified that the blowout was caused by a defect in the manufacture or design of the tire. This expert concluded that the accident was caused when the tread of the tire separated from the steel-belted carcass, and that this separation could be caused from either a defect or from overdeflection, which is a type of tire abuse.

The expert noted that four physical indicators are normally present on a tire when overdeflection is the cause of failure: (1) greater tread wear on the shoulder than in the center of the tire, (2) sidewall deterioration or discoloration, (3) abnormal bead grooving on the tire, and (4) rim flange impressions. When the expert failed to find at least two of these physical elements present, he concluded the failure was not due to overdeflection and therefore must have been caused by a manufacturing or design defect.

Application of the Daubert *Factors*

Defendant sought summary judgment, arguing under *Daubert* that the expert's testimony was inadmissible. The district court applied the four *Daubert* factors, finding first that the expert's methodology was not susceptible to testing because the results were subjective and there was some degree of uncertainty. The district court next found that there were no publications approving or otherwise discussing the expert's techniques for tire-failure analysis. Applying the third factor, the district court found that the potential error rate of the technique could not be determined accurately with the expert's method. As for the fourth factor, the district court found that there was simply insufficient evidence to conclude that the expert's methodology was generally accepted in the relevant scientific community.

The district court concluded that the *Daubert* factors applied whether the evidence was scientific or technical in nature and that those standards had not been met. The district court thus found the expert testimony inadmissible and granted defendants' motion for summary judgment.

Plaintiffs appealed, arguing that the *Daubert* factors did not apply to the admissibility of the expert's testimony because he was not a scientific expert. The Eleventh Circuit agreed, noting that the Supreme Court in *Daubert* limited its holding to the scientific context. The court explained that although *Daubert* may suggest reliability issues for courts to consider under Rule 702, the trial court's role as gatekeeper is not intended to replace the adversary system. The court found that the expert's testimony was not scientific because it relied primarily on his experience in analyzing failed tires.

The Eleventh Circuit reversed and remanded the case for further proceedings, holding that the district court erred as a matter of law when it applied the *Daubert* factors to the expert's testimony.

Supreme Court's Decision

The Supreme Court granted certiorari to determine if and how *Daubert* applied to expert testimony that is not scientific in nature. The Supreme Court reversed the Eleventh Circuit's holding that the *Daubert* factors applied only to the admissibility of scientific expert testimony. The Court held that the gatekeeping function articulated in *Daubert* applied to *all* expert testimony, not just scientific testimony.

The Court explained that the test of reliability is a flexible one, and that *Daubert*'s list of specific factors neither necessarily nor exclusively applies to all experts or in every case. The Court noted that a district court has the same discretionary power under the law to decide *how* to determine reliability as it does with respect to the ultimate determination of reliability. Finally, the Court concluded that the district court acted within its discretion when it decided not to admit the testimony of the expert.

Rationale of the Court   The Court examined the plain language of Rule 702 and determined that it made no relevant distinction between "scientific" knowledge and "technical" or "other specialized" knowledge. The Court explained that the standard articulated in *Daubert* was derived from the language of Rule 702, which indicates no difference between scientific and other types of knowledge.

The Court noted that under the language of Rules 702 and 703, nonscientific testimony is to be given the same "testimonial latitude" as scientific testimony. The Court also recognized that practical application of a rule that created a distinction between scientific and other types of expert testimony would be administratively difficult, if not impossible, to apply. Finally, the Court pointed out that this distinction is ultimately unnecessary because the reason for the rule is to assist the jury in evaluating the expert evidence.

The Court specifically examined the factors that may be used in determining reliability under *Daubert*'s gatekeeping obligation. The decision is clear that the *Daubert* factors may be used by the trial judge to evaluate the testimony of the engineering expert, emphasizing that the application is a "flexible" one.

The Court held that in determining the admissibility of nonscientific testimony, a trial judge may consider the specific factors mentioned in *Daubert* since they might help evaluate the reliability of experience-based testimony. The Court reiterated that it did not intend the *Daubert* factors to be exclusive, but meant them as helpful guidelines, not all of which would be pertinent even in cases involving scientific testimony.

Trial Court's Discretion The Court maintained that a trial judge has discretionary authority to determine whether to admit or exclude expert testimony, and that this discretion is needed to avoid unnecessary reliability proceedings in ordinary cases and to require appropriate proceedings in more complex cases. The Court therefore provided trial judges with broad boundaries to determine an expert's reliability, reiterating that the abuse-of-discretion standard should be used to review a trial court's admission or exclusion of such testimony.

The impact of *Kumho Tire* stretched beyond the judge's role; the ruling heightened the responsibility of litigators to provide evidence of reliability to corroborate their expert's testimony. Litigators also have additional means to attack the credibility of a nonscientific expert witness as unreliable, and this may require more hearings to determine the reliability of an expert.

Effect of the Opinion

The increased scrutiny of nonscientific experts has had the effect of precluding evidence that was often routinely admitted prior to enunciation of the expansive gatekeeper function. But the decision has also opened the door to admissibility of novel evidence that is proven to be reliable. Furthermore, *Kumho Tire*'s expansion of *Daubert* provides trial judges with greater discretion to evaluate expert testimony by permitting the court to examine a multitude of factors beyond those enunciated in *Daubert.* Given the breadth of discretion recognized in *Kumho Tire,* appellate review of lower courts' decisions will of course be highly deferential.

▼▼▼▼▼

The Wider Scope of *Kumho Tire*

"This case requires us to decide how *Daubert* applies to the testimony of engineers and other experts who are not scientists. We conclude that *Daubert*'s general holding—setting forth the trial judge's general 'gatekeeping' obligation—applies not only to testimony based on 'scientific' knowledge, but also to testimony based on 'technical' and 'other specialized' knowledge."

Kumho Tire, 526 U.S. at 141.

The *Joiner* Opinion

Another question left unanswered by *Daubert* was resolved in *General Electric Co. v. Joiner,* 522 U.S. 136 (1997), where the Supreme Court determined the correct standard of review applicable to the trial court's evidentiary rulings. Reaffirming its prior holdings, the Court held that the proper standard of review pertaining to a trial court's evidentiary rulings regarding expert opinions is the abuse-of-discretion standard.

The argument that *Daubert* focused solely on principles and methodology, not simply conclusions, was also addressed. The Court reasoned that conclusions and methodology were not entirely distinct from one another, and thus the abuse-of-discretion review was not confined solely to the methodologies of the expert but to the expert's conclusions as well.

Rules of Discovery 4

THE COMPLEXITY AND THE SIGNIFICANCE of expert testimony have placed a renewed emphasis on discovery matters. The more liberal rules of evidence have placed the burden on the cross-examiner to demonstrate that the basis of the expert's opinion is faulty. And without a thorough knowledge of the expert's opinions, as gleaned through discovery, a lawyer cannot effectively cross-examine the expert.

The Federal Rules of Civil Procedure outline in some detail the discovery parameters of expert witnesses who are expected to testify at trial. The rules provide, among other things, that a party may submit interrogatories and take depositions regarding (1) the subject matter on which the expert is expected to testify, (2) the substance of the facts and opinions asserted by the expert, and (3) a summary of the underlying grounds for each expert opinion. The court may of course order additional discovery and otherwise regulate the timing, scope, and nature of discovery.

Discovery of Consulting Experts

Most discovery rules make an important distinction between consulting and testifying experts. A consulting expert is one who has been retained by a party but will *not* testify at trial. Consulting experts usually educate counsel about the more complicated issues of the case, the trial experts that should be retained, the best way to best present evidence, how to discover, compile, and assimilate data, and so on. If the work-product, opinions, or mental impressions of the consulting expert have not been reviewed by a testifying expert, they are generally not discoverable.

If the budget permits, some lawyers retain two sets of experts—prospective witnesses and consultants. One advantage is that consultants can do much of the preliminary work, thus preventing the release of certain documents and other information.

But you must be careful: Any concealment of facts underpinning testifying witnesses' statements may lead to severe court-imposed sanctions. Another danger is that the more experts one has, the further each one is removed from firsthand knowledge of the case, and therefore the more likely that experts will disagree among themselves. It is also very important that testifying witnesses be able to explain fully how their opinions were reached.

Materials Generated by Consultants

Your opponent is generally not allowed discovery of documents prepared by nontestifying consultants, provided they are not reviewed by a testifying witness. But documents prepared by consultants that are reviewed or otherwise used by a testifying expert are clearly discoverable.

If your expert functions both as a consultant and an expert witness, you must be aware that there is a high risk of disclosure. The court will attempt to protect work-product prepared by an expert performing consulting services only if there is a clear delineation between the two roles.

You should also be aware that if you designate an individual as a testifying expert but decide later not to have the expert testify, the court may still compel the expert to respond to discovery requests.

Protecting the Consultant's Status

To protect the status of a consulting-only expert, it is important *not* to let the consulting expert's work be reviewed by the testifying expert, and *not* to let the consulting expert interact with the testifying expert. Separate files and logs of reviewed documents must be maintained for each expert.

A consulting expert who obtained knowledge about the case either firsthand or in some way other than in consultation about the case is discoverable as a fact witness. Examples include consultants who investigate the scene of an accident or those who were present at the scene when the accident occurred.

Although generally no information from a consulting-only expert is discoverable, the following are examples of exceptional circumstances in which the courts sometimes allow discovery: (1) the object or condition at issue was destroyed or deteriorated after the consultant observed it and before the other party's expert had an opportunity to observe it; (2) there are no other available experts in the same field or subject area; and (3) the withholding party was "shopping" for expert opinions and thus tied up a number of experts under consulting agreements.

Disclosure of Experts

In the usual case, you will have worked with an expert for some time before determining whether that individual will be used as a witness at trial. Until that decision is made, there is no requirement to disclose the identity of the expert or produce other information in connection with the expert's analysis or opinion.

This affords you an opportunity to be educated in the field of expertise, as well as to prepare the expert for the case. In most situations, little is gained by early disclosure of an expert or production of materials relating to the expert's inspection, analysis, or opinions.

Occasionally the parties will informally exchange information about their expert witnesses, but more frequently it will be necessary to seek a scheduling order. Defense counsel should seek an order that requires the disclosure of the plaintiff's experts and the taking of their depositions before the disclosure and deposition of defendant's experts. This gives them the opportunity to know the testimony of plaintiff's experts before subjecting your own experts to deposition.

Dual Role Experts

A party is entitled to the same information about an expert retained to provide both expert testimony *and* consulting advice as for the expert retained only to testify. Unless the producing party can demonstrate a clear distinction between the work done for trial testimony and that done as a consultant, all materials considered by the expert must be produced.

De-Designation of an Expert

An expert who is designated to testify but later de-designated will be considered a consulting-only expert if, before de-designation, no discovery was conducted and the expert did not conduct any tests or examinations. However, a party will be able to conduct limited discovery of the expert if, before de-designation, the facts known and opinions held by the expert were disclosed or the expert conducted tests or examinations.

Discovery of Testifying Experts

Simply stated, a party is entitled to full discovery of the other party's testifying experts. The list below identifies some of the information that can be discovered from testifying experts in initial disclosures and expert reports. More detailed information can be secured by interrogatories, requests for production, depositions, and subpoenas *duces tecum* after the expert report is produced. Local rules may require additional information to be disclosed, so it is always wise to consult those.

Initially a party may request from the other party:

- ◆ Names and addresses of the experts.
- ◆ Topics on which the experts will testify.
- ◆ All data or other information considered by the experts in forming their opinions.
- ◆ Opinions of experts and the basis and reasons for them.

- Copies of reports prepared by the experts.
- Exhibits to be used as a summary of or support for the experts' opinions.
- Current resume and bibliography of the experts.
- List of all other cases in which the experts have testified within the last four years.
- Information regarding the compensation to be paid to the experts.

Materials Authored by Testifying Expert

Federal Rule of Civil Procedure 26, and its state-court equivalents, provides that documents authored by a testifying expert are generally discoverable. The rule also requires production of various expert-generated materials other than documents, such as a videotape created to show how the plaintiff was injured.

Prior Opinions

A party is entitled to obtain the opinions of the testifying expert before his involvement in the underlying litigation. For example, "fact opinions" of a treating physician that are discoverable might include prelitigation notations regarding causation, diagnosis, prognosis, and extent of disability or injury.

Materials Provided by Counsel

Most courts follow the clear language of rules like Rule 26(a)(2)(B) and require disclosure of documents that counsel provides for review by testifying experts. The previous wording that allowed discovery only of documents "relied upon" by an expert has been replaced by a broader standard to include any documents that the expert "considered."

Federal Rule of Civil Procedure 612 provides that if witnesses use a writing to refresh their memory while testifying, the adverse party is entitled to see the writing and use it in cross-examination. The court in its discretion may also require the production of that writing if the witness reads it before testifying.

Courts typically apply the same discovery standard to oral conversations as they do to written materials. Therefore, counsel's memoranda to the file and handwritten notes documenting conversations with an expert are typically discoverable to the extent that the writings were shown to the expert. However, documents used solely by counsel for personal recollection of conversations with the expert are likely to be immune from discovery as work-product reflecting counsel's opinions and strategy.

In other words, any factual information reviewed by a testifying expert will be subject to discovery. Regardless of the extent of influence that the documents have on the expert's testimony, the documents must be made available for discovery.

Contractual Documents

Contractual documents concerning the retaining of a testifying expert by counsel are often discoverable if found relevant to the subject matter. Contractual communications can be also discovered when they are otherwise not available to the requesting party without undue burden and reasonably lead to admissible evidence. You should be especially cautious to not include any information in the contract that might otherwise be privileged.

The moral is clear: Keep written communications between you and the expert to a minimum, and assume that whatever you tell the expert is discoverable. Remember that there is no obligation that the expert write you about anything. It is best not to create potential evidence, particularly that which grows stale with time and becomes more difficult to explain.

Work-Product Protection

If the language of Rule 26(a)(2)(B) is not enough to remove any doubt about the possibility of disclosure of work-product divulged to an expert, the Advisory Committee's comment should be. With regard to the duty to disclose information considered by an expert, the Advisory Committee stated:

> Given this obligation of disclosure, litigants should no longer be able to argue that materials furnished to their experts to be used in forming their opinions—whether or not ultimately relied on by the expert—are privileged or otherwise protected from disclosure when such persons are testifying or being deposed.

Several courts that have found a duty to disclose core work-product divulged to an expert have cited this Advisory Committee note.

The Privilege Dilemma

The federal rules require the disclosure of information considered by expert witnesses in forming their opinions. However, the rules protect attorney work-product by excluding "mental impressions, conclusions, opinions, or legal theories of an attorney" from discovery. Traditionally, communications between counsel and experts that incorporate the attorney's opinions were not discoverable, but those that form the basis of the expert's opinion were.

The core of a Rule 26(b)(4) conflict lies in communications between lawyer and expert that include not only factual information but the lawyer's opinions. Courts are divided regarding what portions of these communications are discoverable, and they have taken inconsistent approaches where applying Rule 26 discovery to communications that incorporate counsel's work-product.

These ambiguities provide little reassurance for lawyers who are trying to protect against unwarranted disclosure. The measures taken to prevent disclosure of such matters are cumbersome and time-consuming, but there are grave consequences for failure to do so.

The Different Approaches

The courts that adopt the broader discovery approach are guided by the general language of Rule 26 and the policy of encouraging liberal disclosure. Under this approach, when material is reviewed by an expert, otherwise privileged work-product of an attorney is discoverable, regardless of whether the information is factual in nature or whether it contains counsel's mental impressions.

Other courts hold that Rule 26 did not create a new standard with respect to opinion work-product, and that the amended rule merely reflects a procedural change to expedite discovery, not broaden the scope of discovery. Under this approach, only the factual portions of communications are discoverable in order to protect counsel's core work-product.

Rule 26(b)(3) divides attorney work-product into two categories: one that is absolutely immune from discovery, and another that is only qualifiedly immune. Fact work-product is sometimes discoverable on a showing of substantial need and inability to replicate the data without undue hardship. Work-product incorporating mental impressions, however, is immune to the same extent as lawyer-client communications when prepared in anticipation of litigation.

Precautions to Prevent Waiver

Regardless of the category of work-product, the privilege can be waived. A growing majority of courts hold that the privilege is waived when counsel provides work-product—whether factual or containing counsel's impressions—to experts who consider it in forming their testimony. Three policy grounds are said to support this disclosure: (1) liberal discovery limits the manipulative control counsel exerts over experts; (2) it does not violate the fundamental precepts of the work-product doctrine; and (3) it actually protects work-product by clearly defining the limits of the doctrine's scope. Not all jurisdictions follow the same thinking with regard to waiver of work-product, so you should exercise the utmost caution, aware that confidential information may be compelled by the court in the most tenuous of circumstances.

Expert Report

An important part of discovery is the expert report. (See Chapter 7 for further discussion.)

Under federal rules, only a retained testifying expert is required to submit an expert report. Nonretained testifying experts—such as in-house experts in a defendant corporation—are not required to submit reports. However, by local rule, order, or written stipulation, the requirement of a written report may be waived for particular experts or imposed on additional individuals who will provide opinions under Rule 702.

The report must be prepared by the expert and written in a manner that reflects the testimony to be given by the expert. Although the lawyer can assist in its presentation, the lawyer should not prepare the report. Under Federal Rule of Civil Procedure 26, the expert report must include the following:

- *Opinions.* A complete (not "preliminary") statement of opinion to be expressed and the basis for it.
- *Data.* A list of the data or other information considered by the witness in forming the opinion. This list should include all materials furnished to the expert for use in forming the opinion, regardless of whether the expert ultimately relied on all of the materials.
- *Exhibits.* Any exhibits used as a summary of, or in support of, the expert's opinion.
- *Qualifications.* The expert's qualifications, including a list of all publications authored in the past ten years.
- *Compensation.* The compensation to be paid to the expert.
- *Other cases.* A list of other cases in which the expert has testified at trial or in deposition in the preceding four years. The list should include enough information for the opposing party to identify and locate each case, such as the case name and number and the court, county, and state where the case was filed.

Advantages of Written Reports

There are several reasons why it may be desirable to have the expert prepare a written report, even if not required. It is a ready reference of the substance of the expert's testimony and a useful summary of the experiments, tests, procedures, and analyses performed by the expert.

A report can also be useful in refreshing the expert's recollection since in many cases a significant amount of time elapses between the time the expert conducts the research and the date of the trial itself. The report can also aid you in structuring the direct examination of the witness and preparing for cross-examination of the opposing expert.

Disadvantages of Written Reports

A number of disadvantages also arise from written reports. A report that contains unfavorable information, or is incomplete in any material respect, can be a potent tool for the opposition. Even if the expert report is essentially favorable, it may provide opposing counsel with a framework from which to prepare an effective cross-examination, and with assistance of the opposing expert, it may be used to reveal deficiencies in your expert's analysis and conclusion. Too, preparation of a formal and detailed report is often very costly.

Precautions for Reports

Care should be taken in the way the report is prepared. Initially, you must provide the expert with all relevant facts. Caution must be exercised in providing any real or documentary evidence relating to the case, because it will likely be discoverable if it forms any part of the basis for the expert's conclusions. Finally, you should instruct the expert to contact you personally or by telephone prior to actually submitting a written report. During this conference, both parties can discuss the report informally to ensure that it contains a minimum amount of irrelevant or damaging information.

The expert should take care to prepare a useful report. The report should contain at the outset a summary of the facts of the case as they are understood by the expert. Any discrepancies that later arise can then be made apparent to you in time to deal with them. Following a recitation of the facts, the expert should respond separately and chronologically to each of the questions you pose. The response should be phrased at the appropriate level of professional certainty. Finally, a summary of the factual and analytical basis for each response should be provided.

A party must supplement an expert report by the deadlines provided in the scheduling order or by the time the party's pretrial disclosures are due, typically 30 days before trial.

Expert Report

Rule 26 of the Federal Rules of Civil procedure states:

> The [expert] report shall contain a complete statement of all opinions to be expressed and the basis and reasons therefor; the data or other information considered by the witness in forming the opinions; any exhibits to be used as a summary of or support for the opinions; the qualifications of the witness, including a list of all publications authored by the witnesses within the preceding ten years; the compensation to be paid for the study and testimony; and a listing of any other cases in which the witness has testified as an expert at trial or by deposition within the preceding four years.

Mandatory Disclosures

The procedural rules of most jurisdictions now require mandatory disclosures early in litigation. The purpose of the mandatory disclosure rule is to accelerate the exchange of information about the case and eliminate paperwork of requesting this information. The federal rules require the parties early on to exchange information about potential witnesses, documentary evidence, damages, and insurance. These disclosures must identify expert witnesses and provide a detailed written statement of the testimony they may offer at trial.

Expert Compensation

Under federal rules, the court may require a party seeking discovery from the opposing party's testifying expert to pay a reasonable fee for time spent in responding to discovery. For depositions, the party seeking discovery ordinarily will pay the expert's fee for the time spent preparing for the deposition, traveling to be deposed, attending the deposition, and returning from the deposition.

In evaluating whether a proposed expert fee is reasonable, courts have typically considered the following factors: the area of expertise; the education and training required; the prevailing rates for comparable experts; the nature, quality, and complexity of the discovery responses provided; the cost of living in the area; the fee being charged by the expert to the retaining party; fees traditionally charged by the expert on similar matters; and any other factor likely to be of assistance to the court in balancing the interests of the parties.

Supplementing Discovery

Most discovery, including expert reports, must be supplemented by the deadlines provided in the scheduling order or by the time the party's pretrial disclosures are due, normally 30 days before trial. A party must also supplement an expert's interrogatories by these deadlines. A party should also supplement its expert report in response to any assertions made by opposing experts that there are gaps in the expert's logic.

Rules of Evidence 5

THE CURRENT PROLIFERATION in expert testimony can undoubtedly be traced to the 1975 enactment of the Federal Rules of Evidence, when Rules 702 through 705 significantly expanded the admissibility of expert testimony. Any expert who is qualified by education or experience can testify as long as the testimony is helpful to the trier of fact. These rules also made it easier to substantiate the basis of the opinion, and they eliminated the necessity of first setting out the underlying facts and data for the opinion. The ultimate-issue restriction was eliminated, as was the requirement for hypothetical questions. The result was to place more responsibility on the cross-examiner to elicit these details on the witness stand.

Fact Witnesses and Expert Witnesses

From a juror's perspective, there may not appear to be a significant difference between testimony presented by fact witnesses and that given by expert witnesses. In both cases the lawyer who conducts the direct examination attempts to demonstrate that

49

the testimony is coming from an unbiased, and therefore reliable, source of information. Only cross-examination reveals to the jury the full extent of the financial relationship between the expert and the lawyer who retains that expert's services.

The evidentiary rules concerning expert witnesses are in many ways more lenient than for fact witnesses. This gives experts several significant advantages.

Practical Advantages of Expert Witnesses

The expert's testimony usually starts with a recitation of the expert's impressive "knowledge, skill, experience, training, or education," as Rule 702 phrases it. Thus, the expert and the lawyer are allowed, and even encouraged, to begin the direct examination with a blatant attempt to impress the jury with the stature of the testimony.

Fact witnesses, on the other hand, can testify only about their observations. Most jurisdictions, including the federal courts, prohibit the presentation of evidence of "truthful character" concerning a fact witness, unless the witness's reputation for honesty has been attacked. While the expert witness can point to specific instances of experience, training, and education in an effort to convince the jury that the testimony is reliable, the fact witness cannot engage in a comparable effort to establish credibility.

Litigators are therefore stuck with the fact witnesses that fate has dealt them. Sometimes completely honest individuals make poor witnesses because they do not express themselves well. Nervousness, personality traits, and a host of other factors can lead jurors to discredit testimony, even if incorrectly. But if the witness on the stand is the only one who can establish a critical fact, the lawyer has no other choice.

There are usually no similar constraints with expert witnesses, for lawyers can choose from among many qualified candidates. The astute lawyer chooses a witness who above all can communicate effectively.

Evidentiary Advantages of Expert Witnesses

Although the practical advantages that experts have over fact witnesses are significant, the most important ones are created by evidentiary rules. Fact witnesses can testify only about their observations, but experts can base their testimony on other facts and data, even those that cannot be admitted into evidence at trial. An expert thus has significantly fewer limitations on the scope of testimony.

There is no doubt that the federal rules, and the states that emulate them, moved the courts toward more liberal admission of expert testimony. For example, the rules no longer prohibit expert testimony based on hearsay, as long as that hearsay is reasonably relied upon by experts in the particular field. Prior disclosure of the facts and data underlying an expert's opinion is no longer mandated. The rules allow hypothetical questions, but they are no longer required. The ultimate-issue rule, which prohibited experts from giving opinions as to ultimate facts in issue, has been abolished.

Admission of Expert Testimony (Rule 702)

Federal Rule of Evidence 702 (and its many state court equivalents) governs the admission of expert testimony. It requires that experts first establish that their testimony will assist the fact finder's understanding of the evidence. Rule 702 does not require that the subject matter be complex; it is only necessary that the expert's testimony assist the jury.

The court must make a preliminary determination under Rule 104(a) that the witness is qualified to give an expert opinion. Under Rule 702, a witness may qualify as an expert by knowledge, skill, experience, training, or education. Thus, anyone with specialized knowledge may qualify as an expert in a particular area.

The clear language of Rule 702 applies to *all* expert testimony. The rule does not distinguish between "scientific," "technical," or "other specialized" knowledge. The Court in *Daubert* ruled that the gatekeeping function was derived from the word "knowledge," not the words that modify it. The legislative history of the rule also supports a broad application of Rule 702 to all types of experts.

Since it was first adopted in 1975, Rule 702 has allowed experts to testify when their "scientific, technical, or other specialized knowledge will assist the trier of fact to understand the evidence or to determine a fact in issue." For almost 20 years, federal courts struggled to interpret Rule 702 because it did not explain *how* to evaluate expert testimony. The Supreme Court, in its 1993 decision of *Daubert v. Merrell Dow Pharmaceuticals, Inc.,* and its 1999 decision of *Kumho Tire Co. v. Carmichael* finally explained how federal courts should apply the rule.

Latest Version of Rule 702

In 2000 Rule 702 was given an important addition, as discussed in Chapter 2. Essentially, Subpart (1) (see "Federal Rule of Evidence 702" sidebar) ensures that experts have adequate reason for reaching the conclusion about which they propose to testify. For scientific testimony, this might include confirming that the expert possesses adequate knowledge about the particular field or has conducted research in the area. For nonscientific testimony, the expert must have had enough experience with, or sufficient study of, the subject of the proposed testimony.

Subpart (2) examines how the expert's conclusion was drawn from the facts or data scrutinized. Even if experts have adequate knowledge of or experience with the subject of their testimony, they must also employ reasonable processes to reach their conclusions. This prong of the rule simply requires that experts reach their conclusions employing the same methodology that they would employ in their professional duties.

Subpart (3) reflects the evolving definition of reliability. Besides requiring witnesses to both have a reliable basis for their opinions and appropriately apply their methods to those facts or data, this subpart requires that the experts' conclusions themselves are a reasonable result of the process and supporting facts.

Instead of listing *Daubert*'s four factors and permitting courts to flexibly apply them, the rule provides general guidance to trial judges about how to apply those—and other—factors. By focusing a trial judge's attention on three aspects of an expert's testimony, the rule provides criteria sufficiently general to address any type of expert testimony.

Helpfulness Standard

If the expert's opinion "will cause the trier of fact to understand the evidence or to determine a fact in issue," as Rule 702 phrases it, the proponent is beyond the first hurdle. Even when jurors are capable of deciding a matter based on their experience, an expert may still have specialized knowledge that will be useful to them as fact finders.

Federal Rule of Evidence 702
Testimony by Experts

"If scientific, technical, or other specialized knowledge will assist the trier of fact to understand the evidence or to determine a fact in issue, a witness qualified as an expert by knowledge, skill, experience, training, or education, may testify thereto in the form of an opinion or otherwise, if (1) the testimony is based upon sufficient facts or data, (2) the testimony is the product of reliable principles and methods, and (3) the witness has applied the principles and methods reliably to the facts of the case."

Rule 702 Cases

U.S. v. Mamah, 332 F.3d 475, 478 (7th Cir. 2003):

"It is critical under [Rule] 702 that there be a link between the facts or data the expert has worked with and the conclusion the expert's testimony is intended to support. The court is not obligated to admit testimony just because it is given by an expert."

U.S. v. Ceballos, 302 F.3d 679, 686 (7th Cir. 2002):

"When a challenge is made to the acceptance or rejection of expert testimony on appeal, we review whether the district court found that the testimony was reliable and relevant *de novo.* If we find that the testimony was reliable and relevant, we review the district court's decision to admit or exclude the testimony for an abuse of discretion."

U.S. v. Finley, 301 F.3d 1000, 1007 (9th Cir. 2002):

Rule 702 "consists of three distinct but related requirements: (1) the subject matter at issue must be beyond the common knowledge of the average layman; (2) the witness must have sufficient expertise; and (3) the state of the pertinent art or scientific knowledge permits the assertion of a reasonable opinion."

Basis of Expert Testimony (Rule 703)

At common law two permissible basis for expert opinions were recognized: the expert could base an opinion on firsthand knowledge (e.g., that of a treating physician), or on facts presented at trial either through the testimony of other witnesses or in response to a properly formulated hypothetical question. In both cases, the facts were clearly identifiable.

Federal Rule of Evidence 703 establishes the permissible basis upon which a qualified expert's opinion may be founded. The rule dramatically expanded the permissible basis for expert testimony. In addition to reliance on facts or data that had been personally observed or made known to the witness at or before trial, an expert may also rely on evidence reasonably relied upon by other experts. The second sentence of the rule (see "Federal Rule of Evidence 703" sidebar) attempts to bring expert witness practice in the courtroom in line with that of experts in their respective professions. It allows an expert to rely on any basis, otherwise admissible into evidence or not, as long as other experts in the field would "reasonably" rely upon that basis.

Much of the information that experts routinely rely on would be admissible in evidence, but the foundation may be difficult or time-consuming to prove. Rule 703 relieves the parties of the onerous burden of parading a large number of witnesses into court to do nothing more than authenticate documents on which the experts have reasonably relied. Instead the rules leave it to cross-examination to reveal any deficiencies or inaccuracies in the basis of the opinion.

Broad Foundational Latitude

Therefore, under Rule 703 an expert may base an opinion on: (1) scientific, technical, and other specialized knowledge derived from education and experience; (2) firsthand out-of-court observation of facts; (3) facts, data, or opinions already admitted, or to be admitted, into evidence and presented to the expert at trial either by hypothetical questions or actual testimony; and (4) facts, data, or opinions not admitted into evidence but presented to the expert outside the courtroom and reasonably relied on by experts in the particular field.

As a result, experts may base their opinions on the statements of others, even though such statements have not been admitted as substantive evidence in their own right. Thus, a qualified physician who testifies as an expert may base an opinion on information related by others who are involved in the patient's diagnosis and treatment, or on information contained in the patient's medical and hospital records. The assumption underlying this change from prior practice is that a qualified expert is competent to assess the reliability of information received from others.

Reliance on Inadmissible Data

The question naturally arises: If otherwise inadmissible data is permitted to explain the opinion, is not Rule 703 a backdoor exception to the hearsay rule and other exclusionary rules?

While it is clear that an expert may *rely* on inadmissible data, it is less clear whether the expert may *recite* that data in support of the testimony. There are three ways in which the courts handle the inadmissible data that forms the basis for an otherwise proper expert opinion. The federal view is to generally prohibit the expert from disclosing the basis. Another view is to admit the basis for the limited purpose of supporting the opinion, but not for the truth of the underlying data. And the third view is to admit the facts supporting the opinion for all purposes.

Thus, under the provision of Rule 703 the witness may refer to the content of any inadmissible documents only if the court determines that their protective value in assisting the jury substantially outweighs their prejudicial effect. Consequently, you and the witness may in certain circumstances want to consider limiting the expert's preparation materials to those that are likely to constitute admissible evidence.

Federal Rule of Evidence 703
Bases of Opinion Testimony by Experts

The facts or data in the particular case upon which an expert bases an opinion or inference may be those perceived by or made known to the expert at or before the hearing. If of a type reasonably relied upon by experts in the particular field in forming opinions or inferences upon the subject, the facts or data need not be admissible in evidence in order for the opinion or inference to be admitted. Facts or data that are otherwise inadmissible shall not be disclosed to the jury by the proponent of the opinion or inference unless the court determines that their probative value in assisting the jury to evaluate the expert's opinion substantially outweighs their prejudicial effect.

Rule 703 Cases

In re Paoli R.R. Yard PCB Litig., 35 F.3d 717, 747 (3d Cir. 1994):

"We have held that the district judge must make a factual finding as to what data experts find reliable . . . and that if an expert avers that his testimony is based on a type of data on which experts reasonably rely, that is generally enough to survive the Rule 703 inquiry."

University of R.I. v. A.W. Chesterton Co., 2 F.3d 1200, 1218 (1st Cir. 1993):

Rule 703 "normally relieve[s] the proponent of expert testimony from engaging in the awkward art of hypothetical questioning, which involves the . . . process of laying a full factual foundation *prior* to asking the expert to state an opinion."

Ultimate Issues (Rule 704)

Federal Rule of Evidence 704 specifically abolished the common-law "ultimate issue" rule, which prohibited experts from testifying on ultimate issues because it was believed that experts would thereby usurp the province of the jury. This does not mean that an expert may always give opinion testimony on ultimate issues, such as whether the defendant was or was not negligent. But it does mean that such testimony will not be automatically excluded.

Rule 704 is not without limits. The use of the expert's opinion must be consistent with Rule 702's "assist the trier of fact" standard, as well as Rule 403's concerns with balancing probative value and the risk of unfair prejudice. Together, these rules safeguard against the admission of testimony that only tells the jury which result to reach and against testimony that is phrased in terms of inadequately explored legal criteria. The rules do not permit an expert to give legal conclusions or to testify as to the principles of law to be applied in the case.

Legal Conclusions

Closely aligned with ultimate issues are those of legal conclusions. As a general rule, an expert may not educate the jury regarding a principle of law or testify to the legal effect of certain conduct. But this general rule has loose boundaries and courts often create individualized exceptions to assist the jury in factual determinations.

Even if experts communicate the proper legal standard, legal conclusions are prohibited because they may interfere with the judge's role of instructing the jury as to the proper standard. Expert statements that a party's actions were "justified under the circumstances," "not warranted under the circumstances," and "totally improper" have usually been held inadmissible because the expert was merely telling the jury what conclusions to reach.

Definitions of Legal Terms

Experts may, however, use terms of art in their nonlegal sense. Thus, experts can use legal words, such as "fraud" and "deceit," provided they are used in the context of their common, ordinary meaning. But an expert's use of legal terms that directly rely on the applicable statutory and regulatory language is suspect and typically disallowed by the courts.

Specialized Aspects of Law

Courts sometimes permit experts to state narrow conclusions of law when the issue involves a statute or provision that is specialized to a particular industry, but legal interpretations that provide more than incidental assistance in understanding that particular technical area of the law will be excluded.

For example, in a patent-infringement action, expert testimony that explains a technical area of the law and provides an opinion regarding the question of infringement may be permitted. The courts in that instance may find no error because sufficient evidence was presented, including the expert's conclusion on infringement, to support the jury's verdict.

▼▼▼▼▼

Federal Rule of Evidence 704
Opinion on Ultimate Issue

(a) Except as provided in subdivision (b), testimony in the form of an opinion or inference otherwise admissible is not objectionable because it embraces an ultimate issue to be decided by the trier of fact.

(b) No expert witness testifying with respect to the mental state or condition of a defendant in a criminal case may state an opinion or inference as to whether the defendant did or did not have the mental state or condition constituting an element of the crime charged or of a defense thereto. Such ultimate issues are matters for the trier of fact alone.

Rule 704 Cases

Burkhart v. Washington Metro. Area Transit Auth., 112 F.3d 1207, 1212–13 (D.C. Cir. 1997):

"[A]n expert may offer his opinion as to facts that, if found, would support a conclusion that the legal standard at issue was satisfied, but he may not testify as to whether the legal standard has been satisfied."

> *Woods v. Lecureux,* 110 F.3d 1215, 1220 (6th Cir. 1997):
>
> "[T]estimony offering nothing more than a legal conclusion—i.e., testimony that does little with more than tell the jury what result to reach—is properly excludable. . . ."

Underlying Facts and Data (Rule 705)

Evidentiary rules like Rule 705 governs the foundational questioning of expert witnesses at trial. The rule breaks ranks with the common law by permitting an expert to give opinion testimony without first testifying to the facts or data underlying the opinion. The rule therefore abandons the requirement that an expert first disclose facts or data underlying the opinion as a prerequisite to admissibility of the opinion itself.

The rule thus abolished the requirement of posing hypothetical questions to the witness who does not have firsthand knowledge of the underlying facts. However, the court retains its discretion to require disclosure of underlying facts or data, or the use of certain types of questioning, when it is appropriate to do so.

The rule contemplates instead that the underlying foundation for the expert's opinion will be elicited on cross-examination, especially since most evidentiary rules permit extensive discovery of an expert's opinions and the basis for those opinions.

Rule 705 dealt with two major objections to the use of hypothetical questions. First, by including only some of the facts introduced into evidence in a complex and often theatrical question, counsel could often mislead the jury, especially since courts had not developed a consistent doctrine regarding the use of hypotheticals. Second, hypothetical questions were often so complex and belabored they wasted time and confused the jury.

The object of Rule 705 is not to eliminate foundational questioning entirely but to ensure that the questions enhance the progress of the trial. The necessity for orderly presentation will often lead to divulgence of much of the supporting data on direct examination.

Potential Hypothetical Issues

The departure from mandating strict hypotheticals does present some problems for cross-examination. The common-law procedure allowed the opportunity to object to potentially inadmissible testimony, but counsel must now be prepared to either second-guess opinions based on unreliable information or wait until cross-examination to discredit the inadmissible testimony.

Most jurisdictions, including the federal rules, do not forbid the use of the hypothetical question as a means of eliciting the opinion of an expert witness. In personal injury litigation the hypothetical question remains an important and useful device by which counsel can summarize the facts of the case in advance of closing argument. In the event that counsel uses a hypothetical question that is improper in form, or is needlessly confusing or prejudicial, the trial judge may require that it be put into a more appropriate form.

The trial court may also invoke a rule like Federal Rule of Evidence 403, which provides that even relevant evidence may be excluded when it carries a danger of prejudice, confusion, or waste of time that substantially outweighs its probative value.

▼▼▼▼▼

Federal Rule of Evidence 705
Disclosure of Facts or Data Underlying Expert Opinion

The expert may testify in terms of opinion or inference and give reasons therefor without first testifying to the underlying facts or data, unless the court requires otherwise. The expert may in any event be required to disclose the underlying facts or data on cross-examination.

Rule 705 Cases

B.F. Goodrich v. Betkoski, 99 F.3d 505, 525 (2d Cir. 1996):

"An expert's testimony, in order to be admissible under [Rule] 705, need not detail all the facts and data underlying his opinion in order to represent that opinion."

University of R.I. v. A.W. Chesterton Co., 2 F.3d 1200, 1218 (1st Cir. 1993):

Rule 705 "deliberately shift[s] the burden to the cross-examiner to ferret out whatever empirical deficiencies may lurk in the expert opinion."

Court-Appointed Experts (Rule 706)

Although not commonly invoked, Federal Rule of Evidence 706 allows the court, on its own motion or that of the parties, to appoint an expert witness. If the expert produces any findings, these will be provided to the parties, and the expert can be deposed and called to testify.

▼▼▼▼▼

Federal Rule of Evidence 706
Court-Appointed Experts

(a) Appointment.
The court may on its own motion or on the motion of any party enter an order to show cause why expert witnesses should not be appointed, and may request the parties to submit nominations. The court may appoint any expert witnesses agreed upon by the parties, and may appoint expert witnesses of its own selection. An expert witness shall not be appointed by the court unless the witness consents to act. A witness so appointed shall be informed of the witness' duties by the court in writing, a copy of which shall be filed with the clerk, or at a conference in which the parties shall have opportunity to participate. A witness so appointed shall advise the parties of the witness' findings, if any; the witness' deposition may be taken by any party; and the witness may be called to testify by the court or any party. The witness shall be subject to cross-examination by each party, including a party calling the witness.

(b) Compensation.

Expert witnesses so appointed are entitled to reasonable compensation in whatever sum the court may allow. The compensation thus fixed is payable from funds which may be provided by law in criminal cases and civil actions and proceedings involving just compensation under the fifth amendment. In other civil actions and proceedings the compensation shall be paid by the parties in such proportion and at such time as the court directs, and thereafter charged in like manner as other costs.

(c) Disclosure of appointment.

In the exercise of its discretion, the court may authorize disclosure to the jury of the fact that the court appointed the expert witness.

(d) Parties' experts of own selection.

Nothing in this rule limits the parties in calling expert witnesses of their own selection.

Rule 706 Case

Quiet Tech, DC-8, Inc. v. Harel-DuBois UK Ltd., 326 F.3d 1333, 1348–49 (11th Cir. 2003):

"[W]e are unfamiliar with any set of circumstances under which a district court bears an affirmative obligation to appoint an independent expert. Quite the contrary, as long as the district court thoroughly considers a request for the appointment of such an expert and reasonably explains its ultimate decision thereon, that decision is vested in the sound decision of the trial court."

Learned Treatises (Rule 803(18))

Learned treatises, books, and articles are often considered reliable because the author has no interest in the particular case before the court, and the work will undoubtedly have been scrutinized by other authorities in the field for accuracy. But the greatest obstacle to substantive admissibility of such treatises is the hearsay rule, which prohibits an out-of-court statement offered for the truth of the matter asserted therein. If the treatise is to be admitted, it has to be accepted as an exception to the hearsay rule.

The federal rules grant learned treatises substantive admissibility under the hearsay exception of Rule 803(18). Typically used for cross-examination purposes, the rule also expands the use of such texts in direct examination of your own witness. Admission under this rule also avoids the unrealistic limiting instructions informing jurors that the contents of the treatise may be considered only for impeachment.

▼▼▼▼▼

Federal Rule of Evidence 803
Hearsay Exceptions; Availability of Declarant Immaterial

The following are not excluded by the hearsay rule, even though the declarant is available as a witness:

. . . **(18) Learned treatises.** To the extent called to the attention of an expert witness upon cross-examination or relied upon by the expert witness in direct examination, statements contained in published treatises, periodicals, or pamphlets on a subject of history, medicine, or other science or art, established as a reliable authority by the testimony or admission of the witness or by other expert testimony or by judicial notice. If admitted, the statements may be read into evidence but may not be received as exhibits.

Reversible Error

When reviewing allegedly improper expert testimony that was objected to at trial, the appellate courts must determine whether the error had "a substantial or injurious effect or influence" in determining the jury's verdict, as they evaluate the severity of the error and the trial record as a whole. The standard of abuse of discretion will be applied, with the court reversing only on a clear showing of abuse and "substantial influence" on the jury's verdict.

A reviewing court will often find the error to be harmless when the expert's allegedly improper testimony is embedded in otherwise unobjectionable testimony in which the jury could have reached the same conclusions as the expert. When the rest of testimony is unobjectionable and the evidence taken as a whole is credible, the error will generally be considered harmless.

You should, however, be aware that you act at your peril by relying on expert testimony for certain legal issues. Expert opinions that venture towards conclusory opinions or ultimate issues of fact are potential grounds for error.

Selecting Experts 6

A FAMILY FRIEND SEEKS your legal advice about an accident that occurred over the weekend. It seems that Tom was using a high-powered nail gun when he drove several five-inch nails into his right thigh. He claims the safety on the gun failed. Before you do anything else, you consider whether an expert will be necessary and, if so, how to go about finding the right one.

After locating several candidates, you must next select who will serve as consulting experts and who as testifying experts. This responsibility should never be undertaken lightly. Retaining effective experts not only increases the likelihood of prevailing at trial but furthers the settlement value of your client's case.

Any expert you retain can expect to be challenged in these areas:

- ◆ Qualifications
- ◆ Bias or interest in the case
- ◆ Reasons for testifying
- ◆ Fees
- ◆ Familiarity with the case

- ◆   Disagreement with conflicting expert authorities
- ◆   Communications with the retaining lawyer
- ◆   Prior testimonial experience
- ◆   Publications

Whether to Retain an Expert

The first consideration is whether the expert would be helpful to the finder of fact. In many cases it may not even be necessary, or even wise, to retain an expert. If a layperson could provide the same proof, the court will undoubtedly disallow such expert testimony anyway.

A common mistake is hiring an expert simply because the opposing party has done so. For example, you have just deposed plaintiff's expert economist in a personal injury action, and she has established a certain sum as the amount of damages for future lost wages. You rush out and hire an economist to testify that lost wages could not be any higher than a certain lower sum. By doing so, you are effectively barred from arguing damages of less than that sum for fear of bringing into question the credibility of your own expert. A better situation in such an instance might be to hire a consulting expert to assist you in countering the testimony of plaintiff's expert with other evidence.

When to Hire the Expert

If the initial review of a case shows that an expert's services will be needed, the question arises: When should the expert be retained? Immediate hiring of an expert sometimes imposes an unjustifiable cost, especially if a quick settlement is a possibility. Early use of an expert may also draw your attention away from other aspects of the case that are equally important. However, because an expert's contributions as an analyst and educator are likely to be useful from the beginning, it is generally advisable to retain one as soon as possible, especially if the case is even the slightest bit complicated.

The sooner experts are retained, the sooner they can assist in gathering and evaluating evidence, identifying claims and potential parties, and determining the need for additional experts. The early selection of experts can also alleviate the possibility that your opponent has retained the best experts in the field, especially if the area of expertise is a narrow one.

Locating the Best Candidates

Selecting the right expert is the biggest challenge of all. An expert in a related field may be able to recommend candidates. Fellow lawyers who have handled similar cases can often make recommendations, and a client in the same field may have suggestions. You should look at directories and Web sites of university faculty and professional societies. The classified advertisements of professional and legal publications may be helpful. If the need for additional experts arises after one has already been retained, the retained expert should be able to suggest others. Lastly, look at other cases in local courts to see who has testified.

When considering candidates, keep in mind the following criteria:

Availability

You should inquire into the expert's ability to commit the time and resources necessary to complete the job. Conveying the amount of work that the expert will have to commit to is critical. Make sure the expert can be depended upon to timely provide necessary information such as reports and to assist with other pretrial matters, and most importantly, that the expert will be available for depositions and trial.

Mastery of the Subject

To perform a teaching function, the expert must not simply be knowledgeable in the field, but have all the facts and theories well-organized and readily available. Knowledge and mastery of the subject—combined with persistence, patience, independence, objectivity, and a questioning mind—make a candidate a good analyst, which is a trait especially useful in the pretrial phases of the case.

Tailored Qualifications

Typically, the testifying expert is chosen because such criteria as credentials, independence, lack of bias, and availability point to the individual as the one who can get the job done. No matter how impressive the expert's qualifications, they must closely match the subject matter of the testimony. An expert may therefore be qualified to give opinions as to some matters, but not others.

Relevant Credentials

If the case involves the explanation of pure concepts, you might be best advised to seek an expert with strong academic credentials who has published in the area. If, on the other hand, the case involves application of technical knowledge, you will no doubt be better off with an individual possessing more practical experience.

Cases involving intricate theory or scientific evidence—where *Daubert* challenges are most likely—will typically require a scientist with strong academic credentials. Cases dealing with large amounts of data will require a computer-literate expert who is capable of organizing and searching data electronically.

Independence

The jury will give your expert's opinion greater weight if they perceive that the expert is independent. While it is reasonable to pay an expert for services rendered, an overly familiar relationship between the expert and the party or its attorney can irreparably damage the expert's credibility.

For similar reasons, you should choose an outside rather than an inside expert. You need an objective voice, and even if your client's choice of an expert who works inside the organization will technically qualify, you should avoid the false economy. (Also look outside for a consulting expert if you are not sure you are getting all the facts from the client.) It is difficult enough to convince a fact finder that an outside expert is objective, and the problem is compounded exponentially by using an inside expert whose testimony is, or at least can be construed to be, tainted by self-interest. Moreover, the other side inevitably will capitalize on your decision by retaining an individual with no such bias. The contrast between experts—which will be clear to all—is likely to be fatal.

Previously Taken Positions

An expert opinion that is in conflict with your position will interfere with your ability to build a credible case. From a resume, it may be difficult to determine whether a potential expert has a deeply ingrained opinion and, if so, how that will affect the case at hand. Previously taken positions are likely to yield a witness who speaks strongly, passionately, and credibly. Ferreting out that belief in advance, however, may not be easy if you are not familiar with the field. It is also important to find out whether the expert has taken a position in his or her advertising.

Residence of Expert

While there is no requirement that the expert reside in the jurisdiction involved in the suit, there may be good reason to choose a local expert. The most obvious one is that the jury may relate more naturally to an individual from the same area. Another consideration is best illustrated by cases where the plaintiff's expert must testify as to the standard of medical care, building codes, and so forth, in the locality. Some states even require that certain experts have practiced within the jurisdiction—yet another reason to always be familiar with the local rules.

In some cases, a local expert may be known in the community and therefore especially authoritative. But a nationally famous expert who lives elsewhere can also prove to be unusually impressive. Bringing in an expert from another part of the country needs to be weighed against the inevitable question about why you had to look outside the region to find an expert. The smaller the specialty or the greater the credentials, the less this is true. The bias in favor of a local expert may be outweighed by a foreign expert's presentation, experience, or reputation.

Courtroom Presence

Probably the greatest intangible factor in selecting an expert is how the individual will appear to a jury. An expert may be outstanding in his or her field and capable of relating that expertise to you in a one-on-one situation but not effective before a jury. You should therefore evaluate the expert's demeanor, impressiveness, and general appearance. Some important considerations include

- Will the expert be comfortable in a courtroom setting?
- Will the expert's manner antagonize a jury in any way?
- Can the expert speak persuasively to the fact finder, using everyday language without sounding condescending?
- How will the expert react to cross-examination?

Ask yourself whether the individual speaks and acts the part of an expert. A polished performance can incite a jury and lead them toward facts and theories you promote. An expert who is too bland, too argumentative, or otherwise unpleasant may repulse a jury and therefore prove detrimental to the case.

The most persuasive expert is credible and confident and possesses that undefinable attribute called "presence." The ability to defend conclusions firmly and calmly, to answer difficult questions, and to appear fair and open-minded cannot be overestimated.

Unimpeachability

All the qualifications of a prospective expert may be rendered moot if the expert can be easily impeached. The prospect of testifying may be so terrifying that the expert stumbles while on the witness stand. A candidate with a history of receiving high fees from the same side of the docket may be perceived as biased. An expert who has taken a position at odds with the one currently espoused had better have a convincing explanation for the change.

Since the expertise and competency of the witness will be tested by the adversary and the court, his or her professional credentials must be impeccable. Determine whether the expert has been involved in any professional disciplinary proceedings. You should also immediately inquire whether the witness has a criminal record, prior testimony, work that is inconsistent with your theory in the case, or a disputed reputation among professional peers. The expert must be beyond reproach, no matter how minor or explainable the matter.

If possible, you should verify the credentials: education; professional licenses and certificates; membership in professional societies; publications; experience in the field; personal information; professional, community, and charitable activities; previous expert testimony; previous litigation or substance of testimony; professional disciplinary actions; criminal record; relationship to the parties, if any; and financial or other interest in the case. Opposing counsel will no doubt conduct such an investigation.

If your expert is not beyond reproach, no matter how minor or explainable the matter, look elsewhere rather than risk the potential adverse impact on the jury.

Other Considerations

- *Professional experts.* Many witnesses lose credibility when they make their living by testifying. A practitioner tends to have more credibility than a professional witness.
- *Expert's history.* Determine if the expert testifies primarily for plaintiffs or for defendants.
- *Fees.* These should be examined for reasonableness and the effect it will have on a jury.
- *Comfort level.* When two experts are reasonably well-qualified, choose the expert with whom you feel more comfortable. Frequent communication and long hours of preparation are necessary to succeed.

Presenting the Case

You now have the delicate and difficult task of discussing with the expert the facts and merits of the case. If you want a totally objective analysis, the situation is simple: You simply ask the expert to give a frank opinion.

But the world is often more complicated than that, and the client's interest usually demands a *favorable* opinion. But retaining an expert who will simply offer the opinion you would prefer will undoubtedly be exposed by the other party. Many experts will color their views to secure employment. It is critical therefore that when you explain to the expert what you need, you structure your presentation in such a way that the expert will understand your desire for an objective view of the situation.

The expert—who at this point is retained only as a consultant and not as a testifying witness—will need time to examine the facts. If the witness then expresses discomfort with the position of the client, you should seek another expert who is more comfortable with the desired approach. But you should always take heed of the first expert's views, which may well indicate a weakness that is taken at your client's peril. In order to advance the client's case, the second expert must be made aware of the first expert's critique.

Early Communications with the Expert

Once a candidate has been located, you must outline the services you expect to be provided. The goals are to (1) establish the expert's role, (2) provide the expert with copies of significant written materials in the case, (3) make arrangements for any necessary examinations, tests, and studies, and (4) agree to the expert's compensation and fees. This preliminary conference can also allow the expert to define and clarify the technical terminology involved in the case.

While a consulting expert is generally not subject to discovery, once the expert is disclosed as a testifying witness, all of your communications with the expert are subject to disclosure. This should be kept in mind at all times.

After you decide to hire the expert, an engagement letter should be sent, defining the role of the expert. This letter may be subject to discovery, so it should not suggest a desired result or provide any facts. Any information sent to the expert should leave the expert open to reaching his or her own conclusions. To that end, do not send summaries of records or depositions, as this severely undermines the independence of your expert. You should also advise the expert not to put any opinions in writing until they have been discussed with you.

Testifying witnesses should be advised that their notes will very likely be requested by the opposition. You should also emphasize the importance of keeping notes that are clear and not subject to misinterpretation.

▼▼▼▼▼

Sample Expert Agreement

May 2, 2005

Re: Four-Wheeler Litigation

Dr. Ed Norfleet
32812 Morgans Creek
Terlingua, TX 78230

Dear Dr. Norfleet:
As you know, this law firm represents Aacme Corp. in litigation relating to four-wheelers. This letter is to confirm your retention by Aacme as a consultant in this matter. We anticipate that you will be working with attorneys from this law firm as well as other counsel representing Aacme.

The work that you are retained to undertake is an essential part of the preparation of litigation and the formulation of litigation strategy. You agree that documents and information of any kind that you (and anyone assisting you) acquire in connection with this matter will be maintained in strict confidence and will not be disclosed to any other person or party without the prior written consent of this law firm or other counsel for Aacme. You (and anyone assisting you) must comply with all protective orders in the litigation. All documentary material provided to you (and to anyone assisting you) together with all copies of it must be returned immediately on request. In addition, any activities that you perform under this agreement and any conclusions or judgments that you reach or have reached must be maintained as confidential. You agree that these restrictions will continue even after the termination of your consulting work in this matter.

You agree not to consult with or engage the service of any other person or entity outside of your organization to assist you with your assignments under this agreement without the prior written consent of this law firm or other counsel for Aacme.

You agree that while the four-wheeler litigation is active, neither you nor anyone assisting you will knowingly accept any engagement to perform other work that is adverse to the interests of Aacme.

Any reports or other documents generated or obtained by you in the course of your work on this matter will be the property of Aacme.

The nature and duration of your retention will be determined by our firm or other counsel for Aacme, and your retention may be modified or terminated by you, this law firm, or other counsel for Aacme at any time for any reason.

Aacme agrees to compensate you for your time at your customary rate of $350.00 per hour ($600.00 per hour for deposition and trial testimony), plus reasonable expenses that you may incur. Significant expenses, i.e., those exceeding $1,000, should be approved in advance when possible. In the event that travel is necessary, we will arrange for you to receive prepaid airline tickets and hotel arrangements, and all hotel expenses will be direct-billed.

Please send your bills to me, and I will forward them to Aacme for direct payment to you.

Of course, nothing in this engagement letter is intended to restrict or hinder you in providing full, complete, and truthful testimony should you be asked to testify in this matter.

Please acknowledge your agreement to these terms in the space provided at the end of this letter and return a signed original to me.

We very much look forward to working with you.

Very truly yours,

J.W. Smith, Jr.

Agreement acknowledged this
_____day of_____, 2005.

_____

Background Materials

It is important to furnish the expert with important factual information at your disposal. This includes the obvious, such as statements of fact witnesses, depositions, interrogatory answers, photographs, and the like. It is far better to err on the side of sending the expert materials that may not be useful rather than omit something that may become important.

The expert should always make the determination of which facts are important to the formation of opinions and conclusions. It is especially important not to create the impression that you are the one selecting the materials given to the expert.

Your expert also should be furnished copies of all relevant pleadings. This will usually include the complaint, answer, counterclaims, and affirmative defenses. This information will be helpful in order to understand the specific issues involved in the case.

Correspondence with the Expert

There will be times when it is necessary to correspond with your expert, but generally it is better to communicate in person or by telephone. Any correspondence sent to an expert can be requested by opposing counsel and used in cross-examination. Be careful what you put in writing.

Letters should be reasonably formal. Do not address the expert by first name, as it creates an impression of excessive familiarity and compromises the appearance of objective analysis. If your expert has a professional or academic title, that should be used.

Correspondence should also be phrased in a neutral manner so as not to suggest conclusions that might compromise the expert. When you forward materials, do not add analysis or comment. If that is necessary, do so by telephone.

Consider closing letters with a sentence thanking the expert for "providing your recognized expertise to analyze the case." This suggests respect for the expert and bolsters the expert's credentials. It may also deter the opposing party from using the correspondence in cross-examination.

Conflicts of Interest

It is a fact of reality: Expert witnesses do not owe their employers the sort of undivided loyalty that lawyers owe their clients. While lawyers are advocates for their clients, expert witnesses are considered independent sources of knowledge who provide opinions to aid the trier of fact. Absent a contract or professional ethical restriction, an expert is generally free to accept concurrent engagements for and against the same party, to concurrently work with and against the same law firm, and to testify against former clients in successive engagements.

An expert's professional freedom is not absolute, however. Agency principles require expert witnesses to reasonably safeguard client confidences and refrain from using confidential information for personal gain or other improper purpose. Contractual provisions between the lawyer and the expert often prohibit employment by the opposing party.

Some professions have enacted ethical codes to prevent or regulate conflicts of interest. For example, the code of professional conduct of the American Institute of Certified Public Accountants states that its members should be free of conflicts of interest and not disclose any confidential client information without the consent of the client. The ethical code of the National Society of Professional Engineers states that its members "should not reveal facts, data, or information obtained in a professional capacity without the prior consent of the client." It also prohibits accepting compensation "from more than one party for services [on or related to] the same project, . . . unless the circumstances are disclosed and agreed to by all interested parties."

Perhaps the greatest constraint on the acceptance of conflicting engagements is a practical one. Expert witnesses depend on references from lawyers to generate business, and those who are disloyal or untrustworthy jeopardize their professional reputation.

Disqualification of Experts

Conflicts of interest involving expert witnesses can be a threat to litigants on both sides of the dispute. A party who shares confidential information with an expert who joins the other side is threatened with exposure of key evidence and even waiver of attorney work-product. A party that obtains its adversary's confidences from an expert may have that expert disqualified, and the lawyers themselves may be disqualified or subject to professional discipline.

Courts generally apply a two-part test to determine whether an expert should be disqualified when hired by the subsequent party. The first question is whether it was objectively reasonable for the first party to retain the expert to believe that a confidential relationship existed. The second question is whether the first party disclosed any confidential information to the expert. In this context, "confidences" refers to something akin to privileged attorney-client communications or attorney work-product. For disqualification purposes, technical information and business information are not considered confidential. The answers to both questions must be affirmative in order to disqualify the witness.

As a matter of policy, courts balance the need to protect opinion work-product and client confidences and to maintain the integrity of the judicial process against the need to ensure that the parties have access to qualified experts. Courts are mindful that if experts are too easily disqualified, lawyers and parties will be encouraged to engage in a race for experts holding adverse opinions and to create an inexpensive relationship with those individuals in order to create a conflict. Such maneuvers threaten the integrity of the judicial process by depriving the courts and parties of qualified expert witnesses.

Precautionary Procedures

From a practical standpoint, courts disqualify experts cautiously because lawyers seeking to invoke a confidential relationship have the knowledge, experience, and ability to avoid conflicts. Thus, lawyers rightfully bear the consequences for failing to take appropriate precautions. A lawyer seeking to retain an expert and establish a confidential relationship should make this intention unmistakably clear and confirm it in writing.

If you provide the expert with materials or correspond with the expert, any work-product should be clearly identified. Before sharing confidential information, you should ask the potential expert to run conflict checks.

"Side Switching"

Expert witnesses retained to testify at trial may offer contrary opinions that favor the opponent. There is no steadfast prohibition against this "side-switching," which is a logical position given the law's treatment of expert witnesses as independent servants of the court who possess opinions and information to aid the trier of fact. Unfortunately, there is little precedent to guide courts confronted with the problems of experts who suddenly realigns their positions.

The issue becomes one of whether the party can withdraw its designation and foreclose the expert's testimony or whether the opponent can subpoena the expert to testify at trial. If the opponent calls the expert at trial, the question is whether the opponent can elicit testimony that the expert was originally retained to provide. Needless to say, an expert's admission that he or she was originally engaged by the opposing party can be devastating.

Standards Applied

Three standards have been applied by the courts to determine whether a party should have access to an adversary's former expert. The first is the "exceptional circumstances" standard in Federal Rule of Civil Procedure 26(b)(4)(B). The second is a "balancing" standard, which weighs the interests of the discovering party against the potential for prejudice to the party who hired the expert. The third and most lenient is an "entitlement" standard, drawn from a few cases holding that a party is entitled to call an adversary's expert notwithstanding the adversary's opposition.

A party's designation of an expert does not always entitle an opponent to depose that expert or to call him as a witness if he switches sides. A party is not allowed to call an adversary's former expert in an attempt to cure the mistake of not designating its own expert. Nor is a party allowed to call its adversary's former expert when the expert's testimony is only indirectly relevant.

A key factor used to determine whether a party should be allowed to compel the testimony of its opponent's former expert is the availability of other expert witnesses. Courts are unlikely to compel an adversary's former expert to testify where there are other available options. The party seeking to compel testimony in that situation cannot claim unfair prejudice if the court precludes the testimony.

If a court compels the testimony of a party's former expert, it will not allow the jury to hear the fact that the expert was once employed by the other party. Evidence of the prior retention is substantially more prejudicial than probative. Jurors hearing such information might reasonably assume that the party who first employed the expert is trying to suppress unfavorable evidence, thus destroying the expert's credibility. If it appears that jurors may still be able to infer how the expert became involved, it may be necessary to exclude the expert's testimony altogether.

In analyzing whether an expert witness should be allowed to switch sides, it is also important to determine whether the lawyer who originally retained the expert shared his or her work-product, mental impressions, litigation strategy, or other confidential information. The expert may be permitted to switch allegiance if the party made no such disclosures. But where such confidences have been revealed, the court is more likely to disqualify the expert.

Expert Compensation

The compensation of expert witnesses typically becomes an issue in two contexts. First, the more expensive the expert, the greater the financial burden on the retaining party and the party seeking to discover the expert's opinions by way of deposition. Second, an expert's income may have a correlation to the expert's willingness to support the theories of the retaining party, regardless of the facts.

Federal Rule of Civil Procedure 26(b)(4)(C)(i) provides that absent manifest injustice, "the court shall require that the party seeking discovery pay the expert a reasonable fee for time spent in responding to discovery." The rule seeks to regulate expert witness fees so that plaintiffs will not be hampered in their efforts to hire quality experts, and defendants will not be burdened by unduly high fees which prevent feasible discovery.

The purpose of the rule is to fairly compensate experts for their time while preventing one party from unfairly obtaining the benefit of the opposing party's expert free of cost. Contrawise, a wealthy party should not be allowed to pay its experts excessively high fees in order to prevent a poorer opposing party from deposing them.

Reasonable Fee Factors

A number of factors have typically been considered by the courts when evaluating the reasonableness of an expert's fee:

- ◆ Witness's area of expertise.
- ◆ Education and training required.
- ◆ Prevailing rates for similar expert testimony.
- ◆ Nature, quality, and complexity of the discovery responses provided.
- ◆ Cost of living in the area.
- ◆ Other factors likely to be of assistance to the court in balancing the interests implicated by Rule 26.

The weight to be attributed to these factors in a given case depends on the circumstances. Applying these factors, the courts will sometimes find the fee exorbitant and reduce it to a more reasonable sum to allow fair access to the other party's experts.

Evidence of Expert's Income

Can an expert be asked about his or her income? An expert's income, whether expressed as a gross sum or limited to litigation-related activities, is considered by some courts to be irrelevant, and in those cases a party is unlikely to be considered prejudiced by its inability to obtain an expert's income information.

Other courts allow discovery of these personal finances, reasoning that while the substantial income that an expert earns from testifying is not necessarily dispositive of bias, it may reveal the expert's financial interest. These courts reason that an expert's income records are within the scope of permissible discovery, but they often restrict such discovery so that it is no more intrusive than necessary.

Chain of Command

Human relations being what they are, the possibilities for interpersonal conflicts between the lawyer and the expert are rife. But there can only be one leader of a trial team, and the expert must not be allowed to prepare the case. The expert should be heard and agreement reached as to how the case will be tried, but it must be made clear that the expert cannot provide strategy. If the expert believes he or she knows how to run the case better than the lawyer, there is potential for substantial disruption.

Presenting Experts 7

YOUR FIRM REPRESENTS the midwestern manufacturer of large farm implements, and word has just arrived that a worker operating a piece of the equipment in Iowa has suffered serious injury while hand-feeding corn into it. You immediately hire experts to look into the allegations of the plaintiff—that the machine was unreasonably dangerous, that its internal mechanisms were moving so rapidly they were difficult to see, and that an "awareness barrier" should have been incorporated into the design.

Where do you go from here in formulating and then presenting the findings of the expert witnesses you retain?

The Gatekeeper Function

When preparing the presentation of expert testimony, keep in mind that the trial judge must ultimately determine whether the testimony has a reliable basis in the knowledge and experience of the discipline under consideration and is relevant to the facts at hand.

Federal Rule of Evidence 702 was not designed to disqualify certain classes of expert testimony, but focused instead on the methodology of the expert. Because the courts possess such broad discretion, the outcome of most cases will depend heavily on the determination made by the judge in a hearing that determines the admissibility and pretrial discovery of experts.

By focusing a trial judge's attention on three aspects of an expert's testimony, Rule 702 provides criteria sufficiently general to address any type of expert testimony. Although its criteria remain flexible, the rule ensures that litigants know the general expectations of judges during a pretrial reliability hearing.

▼▼▼▼▼

Federal Rule of Evidence 702

If scientific, technical, or other specialized knowledge will assist the trier of fact to understand the evidence or to determine a fact in issue, a witness qualified as an expert by knowledge, skill, experience, training, or education, may testify thereto in the form of an opinion or otherwise, if (1) the testimony is based upon sufficient facts or data, (2) the testimony is the product of reliable principles and methods, and (3) the witness has applied the principles and methods reliably to the facts of the case.

Foundation of the Opinion

When an expert's testimony is based on facts or data that the witness obtained outside the courtroom, the trial court must make a preliminary determination as to whether the foundations on which the witness relied are of a type that experts in the field reasonably rely on.

Unlike fact witnesses, expert witnesses are under no obligation to restrict opinions to matters personally observed. Instead, Rule 703 explicitly states that the personal-knowledge requirement is not applicable to experts. The rule outlines the almost limitless potential basis for expert opinions:

> The facts or data in the particular case upon which an
> expert bases an opinion or inference may be those perceived

by or made known to the expert at or before the hearing. If of a type reasonably relied upon by experts in the particular field in forming opinions or inferences upon the subject, the facts or data need not be admissible in evidence.

Under this rule, these facts and data can include inadmissible hearsay, privileged communications, otherwise irrelevant information, and other inadmissible evidence.

▼▼▼▼▼

Federal Rule of Evidence 703

The facts or data in the particular case upon which an expert bases an opinion or inference may be those perceived by or made known to the expert at or before the hearing. If of a type reasonably relied upon by experts in the particular field in forming opinions on inferences upon the subject, the facts or data need not be admissible in evidence in order for the opinion or inference to be admissible. Facts or data that are otherwise inadmissible shall not be disclosed to the jury by the proponent of the opinion or inference unless the court determines that their probative value in assisting the jury to evaluate the expert's opinions substantially outweighs their prejudicial effect.

The trial court may resolve the issue either *in limine* or at trial. The court must make an independent assessment, based on a factual showing, that the material in question is sufficiently reliable for experts in that field to rely on it. It is not sufficient for the court simply to ascertain that other experts do in fact rely on that type of facts or data.

Therefore, experts may base their opinion on (1) scientific, technical, and other specialized knowledge derived from education and experience; (2) firsthand out-of-court observation of facts; (3) facts, data, or opinions already admitted, or to be admitted, into evidence and presented to the expert at trial either by hypothetical questions or testimony; and (4) facts, data, or opinions not admitted into evidence but presented to the expert outside the courtroom and reasonably relied on by experts in the particular field.

Practice Pointers

◆ Insist that the expert visit the war room and handle the documents

◆ Keep the nontestifying expert separate from the testifying expert. The nontestifying expert may have some good ideas about ways to present and win the case, but if he or she communicates those ideas directly to the testifying expert, the nontestifying expert may become part of the basis for the testifying expert's opinion and therefore subject to discovery.

◆ Explain the relevant law, including the *Daubert* standards, to the expert. Experts need to know whether their opinions are going to be judged by particular legal standards.

◆ Review the most helpful and the most harmful documents with the expert witness.

◆ Remind the expert not to be an overt advocate. If during a deposition or trial testimony, the expert refuses to concede reasonable points or to recognize limitations or exceptions to the expert's testimony, then the expert's credibility will be diminished.

Issue Identification

Once an expert has been engaged, your first task as lawyer is issue identification. Even good lawyers can miss issues that are easily recognized by a skilled expert in the field. Therefore, you should encourage the expert to consider or investigate relevant issues beyond those that you have first identified. You should, however, advise the expert not to delve into investigation of all topics, however interesting, because some may be legally irrelevant or otherwise foreclosed. The expert must understand that the legal system often requires that issues be approached from a particular perspective.

The key is good communication between you and the expert. This should be a constant process, with the expert regularly informing you of findings and inquiries and with you matching the expert's work to the issues of the case.

As the litigation proceeds, it will eventually be necessary to concentrate the expert's work. At some point you will have to determine which issues are most relevant and which are to be discarded. Ultimately, the expert must be provided with a definitive statement of issues to be addressed.

Providing Information to the Expert

This caveat is of primary importance: Assume that whatever you tell the expert about the case will be discoverable. Since it is impossible to predict how a particular judge will rule on the issue of waiver of attorney work-product, the best strategy is to disclose it only to your client and your trial team and to provide the testifying expert only with nonconfidential information.

Admission of Bad Facts

It makes sense when you think about it: Experts must know the bad facts, so they can analyze and explain those facts in ways that are consistent with your theory of the case.

The lawyer usually begins by giving the expert a brief outline of the facts, but with time the expert eventually acquires a substantial body of documents, exhibits, and other data. Determining what information to provide the expert is one of your biggest challenges, especially when many documents are involved, as is often the case. Providing the expert with practically every document available can be problematic in complex cases.

You should never fail to provide an expert with an important document, and one never knows which document might turn out to be the key to the case. The expert, however, should not be expected to wade unaccompanied into an endless array of undifferentiated documents. On the other hand, experts are often given too few documents, and they should be encouraged to bring that problem to your attention.

Federal Rule of Evidence 703 makes it clear that the basis for expert testimony must be information that is considered reliable by persons working in the field. The expert must be the one to decide what information to consider. In response to the question at deposition or cross-examination about who selected the information considered, the expert must be able to truthfully reply, "I did."

Materials Supplied by the Lawyer

There are certain types of information that an expert will inevitably want to receive from you in the beginning:

- ◆ Chronology of events
- ◆ Names, positions, and roles of important witnesses
- ◆ Prior statements of every witness whose testimony may be germane to the expert's opinion
- ◆ Names of opposing experts, their testimony, data and information they used, assumptions they made, and scientific methods employed
- ◆ Names of opposing counsel and any pertinent information
- ◆ Opposing party's position in the case and the factual basis for the opposing party's claim or defense
- ◆ Any facts that might undermine or detract from your expert's opinion

The sooner you can provide this information to the expert, the better.

Examinations, Tests, and Studies

One of the most useful services that an expert can perform is to conduct various examinations, tests, and studies. To be certain that these are completed within the necessary timeframe, arrangements should be made at the earliest possible moment.

The expert should be capable of explaining the results and the relevance of each study or test and should have some opinion as to their validity and acceptance in the field. If conditions under which these studies were conducted were not ideal, you must inquire why, since the opponent certainly will. If the discrepancy is damaging to the expert's work, it may be best not to use the evidence at trial.

The expert may also be able to refer you to outside supporting or rebutting studies. If the results are not consistent, there may be a reasonable explanation. This is of course likewise true with regard to the findings of the opposing expert.

The expert should be as thorough as possible under the circumstances in preparing opinions for discovery, deposition, and trial. Exhaustion of all possible tests and procedures may not be required, but the expert should be prepared to justify any omissions. The expert should also inform you of any unfavorable information developed by the analysis.

Team Approach

An initial investigation by consulting experts often reveals the need for additional experts to study certain aspects of the case. When assembling such a team, you must pay careful attention to the interaction among testifying experts.

Individual experts may develop preliminary opinions inconsistent with each other, and these unfavorable opinions could become discoverable if one of the consulting experts is later designated as a testifying expert. Therefore, the experts should initially communicate with you and not one another. Once you have a good understanding of each expert's analysis, you can allow direct communication among the testifying experts.

Duty of the Offering Party

The party offering the expert testimony has the burden to show that the expert possesses the proper educational background or requisite experience to qualify as a person with specialized knowledge, that the expert's methodology is reliable, and that the opinion expressed is relevant to the facts at hand.

A lack of specialization does not affect admissibility of the expert opinion, only the weight to be given to it. As long as some reasonable assurance of qualification is offered, the testimony can be admitted, with the expert's qualifications becoming an issue for the trier of fact, not the court.

To ensure that the expert's opinion is reliable, it is necessary to show that relevant factors of reliability support admission of the evidence. For example:

> *Studies.* The opinion espoused must be supported by objective empirical studies. Any articles or empirical data that are damaging to the expert's methodology should be specifically addressed, distinguished, and discredited. In some instances, novel theories will not have been published or subjected to peer review. Lack of peer review is not dispositive if expert's opinion is supported by widely accepted scientific knowledge.

> *Testing.* Experts must show that they have tested the opinion espoused. This factor does not apply when the expert did not perform original research, but instead only surveyed the available literature and arrived at conclusions different than the literature.

> *Data.* The opinion espoused must be supported by sufficient facts or data. These may include inadmissible evidence, hypothetical facts, and other experts' opinions. When reviewing the sufficiency of the underlying facts, the court must determine whether the expert considered enough facts to support the opinion. The reliability of the underlying data generally goes to the testimony's weight and not its admissibility.

> *Error rate.* The potential rate of error for the opinion espoused must be proven to be low.

> *General acceptance.* The opinion espoused must be shown to have gained general acceptance in the expert's discipline. If the scientific evidence is not generally accepted, *Daubert* and *Kumho Tire* allows for its admission as long as its reliability has other independent support. Experts may properly rely on a wide variety of sources of information and may employ a similarly wide choice of methodologies in developing an opinion.

> *Other factors.* In addition to explaining why some or all of the factors set forth in *Daubert* do not apply, the expert opin-

ion should address any other concerns raised by the opponent and explain what other factors would be appropriate
based on the facts and expertise at issue. The principal focus
is the expert's methodology, which should reveal the same
level of intellectual rigor as that of other experts in the field.

Application of the methodology. The reasoning and methodology must be shown to have been properly applied to the
facts and can assist the trier of fact in resolving an issue.
An expert's testimony need not relate directly to the ultimate issue to be resolved by the trier of fact; it only needs
to be relevant in evaluating a factual matter.

Expert Reports

Federal Rule of Procedure 26 requires that retained testifying
experts prepare a written report. Even in jurisdictions where it is
not required, a report proves helpful for both the expert and the
fact finder in that it serves as a cogent summary of the expert's
findings. The disadvantages, of course, are its intractability and
its often detrimental use by the opposition.

In preparing a report the expert must remember a few important things: The report must be timely and complete; the report
must primarily be the work of the expert; and the report must be
properly supplemented and corrected as information or analysis
changes. Attempts by the expert to introduce new theories or
approaches (and new data and methodologies through rebuttal
reports) will no doubt be quickly admonished by the court.

Report Contents

Under the federal rules, the expert report must include the
following:

- Complete statement of all opinions to be expressed by the
  expert.
- Basis and explanations for the opinions.
- Data or information considered in forming the opinions.
- Exhibits to be used as a summary of or in support for the
  opinions.

- ◆ Qualifications of the expert, including a list of all publications in the preceding ten years.
- ◆ Compensation to be paid to the expert.
- ◆ Listing of any other cases in which the expert has testified at trial or in deposition within the preceding four years.

Expert Report Pointers

A few other points regarding expert reports are noteworthy:

- ◆ In writing reports, experts should be aware that their notes and preliminary drafts may be subject to discovery.

- ◆ The inclusion of material in a report does not preclude questioning on that and other material at a deposition.

- ◆ It is proper to inquire at a deposition about the process leading to the production of the expert report. If the lawyers have participated too actively, not just by reviewing and correcting drafts but by materially writing the report, a court may strike all or part of the report and even prevent the expert from testifying.

- ◆ Before an expert's list of credentials is produced, review it in detail with the expert and ask for an explanation for each entry. Professional and educational affiliations should be stated accurately, coauthored works identified as such, and so forth. Pay attention to any omission or ambiguity that could later cause embarrassment.

Suggested Format

The federal rules do not mandate a particular format for the report. While the minimal purpose is simply to inform the other side of the substance of the expert's opinion, it is usually preferable to write a narrative report that makes the expert's opinion readily understandable. An expert's report is not a technical document directed to other professionals in the expert's field, but is intended to be read and comprehended by the lawyers in the case, and perhaps by the judge and jury as well.

Most expert reports begin with an introductory segment, including a summary of the expert's qualifications. The report then sets out a clear and comprehensive statement of the expert's ultimate conclusions. The expert next explains the theory or summary underlying the opinion, and then the analysis and thought processes used to reach the conclusions. Finally, the report lists supporting data or documents. Thus, the broad outline of the expert's report might read as follows:

> *Introduction.* A brief statement of the expert's involvement in the case, including the summary of the expert's most salient qualifications.
>
> *Procedures performed.* A short description of the procedures performed by the expert and the sources of information relied upon.
>
> *Statement of opinion.* A concise statement of the expert's ultimate conclusions in the case.
>
> *Overview.* An explanation as simple as possible of the theory or process underlying the opinion.
>
> *Analysis.* The longest section of the report, explaining why the expert chose a certain approach and detailing the step-by-step process of analysis or application. Depending on the nature of the case, this section may include tables, summary charts, or other exhibits.
>
> *Supporting data.* Information that may be difficult for a lay reader to understand, therefore placed at the end of the report or in a separate section.

Many of the necessary components of a report may be submitted as attachments or appendices, which is preferable because it allows the reader to consult those sections if interested.

Before drafting the report, the expert should discuss its precise scope with you. This allows the expert to deal with legally significant issues and discuss them in the context of pertinent legal standards. As a result, you may want to instruct the expert whether to address certain issues and to critique the opposition's theory.

▼▼▼▼▼

Sample Expert Report

IN THE UNITED STATES DISTRICT COURT
FOR THE NORTHERN DISTRICT OF TEXAS
DALLAS DIVISION
Case No. 0-000-000

AAA Corporation,
Plaintiff

vs.

BBB Corporation
Defendant

EXPERT REPORT OF JOHN DOE

I have been asked to evaluate the economic damages, if any, suffered by AAA Corporation ("AAA") related to its claims in the above referenced matter resulting from the alleged patent infringement by BBB Corporation ("BBB"). AAA has asserted BBB infringed its U.S. Patents No. 0001 and 0002. In general terms, the inventions and teachings in these patents relate to food preservatives. For my work in this matter, I have assumed that the patents-in-suit are valid, enforceable, and infringed by BBB. Due to the fact that AAA has not been engaged in the business of manufacturing or distributing food preservative products and services during the infringement period, the appropriate measure of economic damages, if any, in this matter is no less than a reasonable royalty. This is in accordance with the patent damages statute, 35 U.S.C. § 284.

This report summarizes my opinions, findings, observations, and conclusions to date. It is my understanding that discovery in this matter is ongoing. Therefore, I may modify this report or update my opinions, analyses, or conclusions subsequent to the date of issuance of this report.

I.   Qualifications

  1. I am vice chairman and a managing director of . . . . Prior to that time, I was a partner with . . . .

2. I have been a consultant to a wide range of business organizations. As part of my consulting activities, I have served as an economic and licensing consultant and expert in lawsuits on a variety of issues in different industries. I have conducted numerous studies of patent licenses, licensing strategies, and damages in patent infringement and other consulting engagements. A copy of my current curriculum vitae summarizing my experience and qualifications, including my current and past employment, professional affiliations, publications over the past ten years and testimony over the past four years, is presented in Exhibit 1.

3. I have billed AAA for my work on this case at my customary rate of $400 per hour. My fees are not contingent upon the outcome of the litigation.

II.   Procedures Performed and Documents Relied Upon

4. In developing my opinions in this case I, and staff working under my direction and supervision, have obtained information from documents produced in this matter, interviews with AAA personnel, transcripts of depositions, and review of third-party source material. The sources of information relied upon in forming my opinions are listed in Exhibit 2 to this report. Review and analysis of this information performed, together with my experience and knowledge in this area, has formed the basis for my opinions.

III.   Summary of Opinions

5. AAA is not a manufacturer or seller of food preservative products intended for public consumption. Therefore, the measure of compensation for the alleged patent infringement by AAA is no less than a reasonable royalty. A reasonable royalty is generally considered to be the compensation that the parties would have agreed should be paid to the patent holder by the infringer if a negotiation were held as of the date of first infringement.

6. To determine the appropriate compensation to be paid to the patent holder, various factors must be considered, including the appropriate royalty structure, the date(s) of the hypothetical negotiations, the royalty base, the royalty

market factors and the expectations of the parties regarding the market, and the infringer's historical and projected sales as of the date(s) of the hypothetical negotiation(s).

7. Based on my review of the BBB license agreements made available as of the date of this report, it is BBB's practice to enter into broad, nonexclusive, royalty-free cross licenses that may include a balancing payment. The licenses reviewed also may include provisions for renegotiations of the licenses after a five-year period, allowing for changes in market conditions and prevailing technologies.

8. Due to the fact that AAA, unlike BBB, is neither a manufacturer nor distributor . . . .

9. With respect to the 0001 and 00002 patents, it is my understanding that . . . .

10. BBB is alleged to have infringed . . . .

11. It is my opinion that AAA would have been willing to enter into a hypothetical negotiation . . . .

12. Based on BBB's apparent willingness to provide for a five-year renegotiation . . . .

13. It is my understanding that AAA filed its original complaint in this matter . . . .

14. In summary, it is my opinion that three hypothetical negotiations would have taken place between AAA and BBB in 1987, 1992, and 1997. A variety of factors would have been considered in each hypothetical negotiation, including the potential benefits to BBB from access to the patents-in-suit, its costs to "design around" the patents, and the prevailing conditions in the market. It is my opinion that the license agreements reached in the hypothetical negotiations between AAA and BBB in 1992 and 1997 would have resulted in lump-sum royalty payments of approximately $21 million and $54 million, respectively, resulting in total royalty payments of $75 million. This does not include any consideration of AAA's opportunity cost.

IV. **Background Summary**

A. *AAA Corporation*

15. AAA was incorporated in 1958 and is headquartered in . . . .

16. In 1984, AAA was reorganized into four principal business areas . . . .

17. AAA is also the leading designer, manufacturer, and distributor . . . .

B.   *BBB Corporation*

18. BBB was founded in 1968 . . . .

19. BBB's U.S. operations are based in . . . .

20. In 1992, it was clear that BBB was aware of the increasing importance of . . . .

21. In 1995, BBB's joint venture with . . . .

C.   *Patents at Issue*

22. The inventions in the patents-in-suit are as follows:

0001 Patent

23. The 0001 patent, issued on . . . .

24. The patent seeks to . . . .

0002 Patent

25. The 0002 patent, issued on December 11, 1978, is directed to improving the quality . . . .

26. The patent seeks to . . . .

V.   **Reasonable Royalty Analysis**

Framework for Hypothetical Negotiations

27. According to 35 U.S.C. §284, "Upon finding for the claimant the court shall award . . . ."

28. The essence of the guidance ". . . to determine an amount adequate to compensate for the infringement . . ." is to evaluate what would have resulted if the patent holder . . . .

Royalty Payment Structure

29. Most of the AAA and BBB license agreements produced in this litigation are broad, royalty-free cross licenses. Lump-sum balancing payments were made . . . .

30. Compensation in the form of lump-sum payments serves to benefit both parties . . . .

31. I also reviewed and analyzed a combination of . . . . BBB's infringing sales were projected for the . . . .

32. I also assessed factors relevant to a determination of a range of reasonable royalty rates . . . .

A.   *Industry Licensing Practices*

AAA Licensing Policies

33. Based on discussions with current and former AAA licensing executives and consultants, it is my understanding that . . . .

34. In its 1990 10-K filing, AAA's management acknowledged the value of its patent portfolio stating that . . . .

35. Further underscoring the importance of its licensing program, AAA's management stated in its 1997 10-K filing that . . . .

36. Based on my analysis of the license agreements available for review as of the date of this report, AAA entered into numerous license agreements . . . .

37. During the period from 1995 through 2000, AAA also completed negotiations of . . . .

38. It is my understanding that AAA typically attempts to first initiate contact with alleged infringing parties . . . .

39. I considered license agreements negotiated by AAA in my determination of a reasonable royalty payment . . . .

BBB Licensing Policies

40. It is my understanding that BBB began its initial licensing activity in 1980, at which time it emphasized obtaining and licensing patents deemed "essential" to . . . .

41. BBB, however, modified its licensing policy around . . . .

42. In its 1992 20-F filing, BBB underscored the importance of its licensing activities . . . .

43. In July 1990, BBB created a formal business unit . . . .

44. My analysis of BBB's license agreements made available as of the date of this report serves to corroborate this practice. The majority of BBB's patent licenses are . . . .

45. Of the various licenses entered into by BBB, I found . . . .

B.   *Determination of the Royalty Base*

46. It is my understanding that two broad groups of products designed, manufactured, and marketed by BBB are accused of infringing the patents-in-suit. The infringing product groups include . . . .

47. The 0001 and 0002 patents, as described earlier, contain novel features. It is my understanding that . . . .

48. I have been asked to assume that . . . .

49. With the introduction of its products into the U.S. market, BBB . . . .

C.   *Projections of Sales as of the Hypothetical Negotiation Dates*

50. In order to establish the hypothetical royalty base, I reviewed certain documents in order to determine BBB's expectations about the alleged infringing product sales at the time of each hypothetical negotiation. These included . . . .

1988 Hypothetical Negotiation

51. As previously discussed, in my opinion a hypothetical negotiation would have taken place in 1988 . . . .

1990 Hypothetical Negotiation

52. This negotiation would have focused on the 0001 patent and would have resulted in a five-year license . . . .

53. In calculating the royalty base . . . .

54. Based on the above, I calculated a total royalty base of approximately . . . .

D. *Market-Comparable Approach to Royalty Analysis*

55. An approach I would generally consider useful in assessing the structure of a license agreement and the amount of a potential payment in a hypothetical negotiation is the market-comparable approach. Publicly available sources were searched . . . .

E. *Georgia Pacific Factor Analysis*

56. A determination must be made regarding royalties that would have been negotiated at the time of the alleged infringement. Frequently, this determination of reasonable royalties is . . . .

57. The first step in a *Georgia-Pacific* analysis is to determine the date of first infringement. In this matter, the first infringement of the patents-in-suit . . . .

VI. Conclusion on Reasonable Royalties

58. The following describes the calculation of the lump-sum royalty payments that would have resulted from the hypothetical negotiations in 1992 and 1997:

1992 Hypothetical Negotiation

59. It is my opinion that the 1992 hypothetical negotiation would have resulted in a royalty rate of . . . .

1997 Hypothetical Negotiation

60. It is my opinion that the 1997 hypothetical negotiation would have resulted in a royalty rate of . . . .

Reasonable Royalty Conclusion

61. Based upon my analysis of the factors discussed throughout this report, and my experience in the licensing area, it is my opinion that the 1992 and 1997 hypothetical negotiations between AAA and BBB for licenses to the patents-in-suit would have resulted in lump-sum royalty payments totaling . . . . See Exhibit 3.

VII. Reasonableness of Royalties

62. In conjunction with my determination of the royalty payment due to AAA, I have performed additional analyses to demonstrate the reasonableness of the calculated lump-sum royalty payments as follows:

Running Royalty Option

63. I considered the impact of the application of the determined royalty rates discussed above to AAA's actual reported U.S. sales. This allowed for comparison of the calculated lump-sum royalty payments to . . . .

64. For the period from August 1992 through 1996, AAA's actual U.S. sales . . . .

Sales and Profitability of Accused Products

65. I also considered the calculated lump-sum royalty payments relative to BBB's actual reported total sales and profitability in connection with the accused products . . . .

66. For the period from August 1992 though 1999, BBB's actual U.S. sales of . . . .

67. Collectively, the calculated lump-sum royalty payments due for the period from August 1992 through 1999 totaled approximately . . . .

VIII. Conclusion

68. Based on the documents reviewed, my analysis of the information related to this case, and my experience and background, I have concluded that AAA has sustained damages in this matter of approximately . . . .

69. This report may be modified or amended if additional information comes to my attention after the date of this report. My work in this matter and the opinions expressed in this report are based on the documents reviewed and analysis performed through the date of this report.

Respectfully submitted,

_____   _____
John Doe   Date

Motions in Limine

If admissibility of your expert is not reasonably certain, you should consider seeking a pretrial ruling on the standards to be applied to experts through a motion *in limine*. If the court adopts a specific criteria for qualifying witnesses, at least you have the opportunity to lay a proper foundation. If that judicial determination is not made until trial, preparation on your part is virtually impossible. A carefully worded motion *in limine* should call to the court's attention any matters that might bar the witness's testimony altogether.

Resisting Gatekeeper Proceedings

Your opponent will no doubt raise objections to your expert, and it is your job to resist those objections. In short, you must argue that gatekeeper proceedings are necessary because (1) your expert and the methodology are proper on their face and (2) it is the role of the fact finder to judge the weight and credibility of the expert's testimony. A supplemental affidavit from the expert can be offered to clear up any objections.

You should initially argue that full gatekeeper proceedings are not required because this is an ordinary case in which the reliability of the expert's methods are proper on their face and the expert's reliability has not been called sufficiently into question. You should also argue that the court's role as gatekeeper is not intended to replace the adversary system, and that the *Daubert* decision noted that vigorous cross-examination, presentation of contrary evidence, and careful instruction on the burden of proof are the traditional and appropriate means of attacking even questionable evidence.

If you are unsuccessful in your attempts to stop the gatekeeper proceedings from going forward, you should emphasize that the focus of the gatekeeper analysis should be on principles and methodology, not the conclusions that they generate. Whether your expert might have done a better job is similarly irrelevant.

Affidavit in Support of Expert

Because you bear the burden of proving that your expert's opinion is both reliable and relevant, you should support your response with the expert's affidavit. If the expert has already been deposed, a supplemental affidavit may be offered to clarify any ambiguous or confusing deposition testimony. At the very least, the affidavit should specifically set forth the following information:

- ◆ The expert's opinions.
- ◆ An explanation of the bases for the expert's opinions, and precisely how the expert reached these conclusions without any logical gaps.
- ◆ Evidence of methodology, or how the opinions are the result of the same level of intellectual rigor as would be used in the expert's field. If applicable, the expert should show that the same method has been followed by at least a recognized minority of experts in the field. This should be supported by a list of objective sources (e.g., learned treatises, policy statements of a professional association, or published articles in a reputable journal demonstrating the accepted methods in that field).

In *Kumho Tire,* the Supreme Court indicated that full gatekeeper proceedings are unnecessary in ordinary cases when the reliability of an expert's methods is properly taken for granted, but may be necessary when reliability is "called sufficiently into question."

It is not clear what the movant must show to call reliability into question. The trial court has the discretion to determine what proceedings are needed to investigate reliability. In determining admissibility, the court is not bound by the rules of evidence except those governing privileges.

Burden of Proof

Once a party objects to your expert's testimony, you bear the burden of proving by a preponderance of the evidence that the expert's opinions are reliable. However, you do not bear the burden of proving that those opinions are correct. In other words, you do not have to show that you will win or lose its merits—only that the evidentiary rules have been satisfied.

Jury Selection

You should begin by asking the prospective jurors if they have heard of any of the experts. Besides identifying any bias or conflicts of interest, this builds expert credibility even before the testimony is presented. The mere mention of the individual's expertise conveys the message that the expert is important. Identifying the expert's specialty and a brief explanation of that specialty further enhances credibility.

Opening Statement

In your opening statement, you should explain the necessity of using experts as well as the reason for selecting particular witnesses. By doing so you enhance the credibility of the witness in the eyes of the jurors.

You should also prepare the jury for conflicting expert opinions. You can then briefly describe why the testimony of your expert is more relevant and reliable.

Next, you should summarize the testimony of the opposing party. This prepares the jury for the differences in the opinions. Render the differences between experts into qualifications for your experts.

If your expert is from out of town, disclose that to the jury early on. You may want to explain that the expert was brought in because an expert with outstanding credentials could not be found locally. This will take the wind out of your opponent's argument about your "having" to search for an expert.

Introduction of your expert witnesses during the opening statement should include a very brief statement of their qualifications to impress the jury with their credentials.

Any deficiencies in the case relating to the experts should also be explained to the jury. This will deprive opposing counsel of his or her thunder. Anticipate any other issues that will occur on cross-examination and mention those as well.

If your own cross-examination includes an aggressive attack on the credibility of the opposing experts, tell the jury that you will be forced to engage in an exchange that is less courteous than you would prefer. Explain that this is necessary to elicit all of the facts of the case. This will prepare the jury for the antagonism. The jury will also appreciate your candor and your need to be forceful.

Preservation of Error

Preserving error is of course vitally important. Keep these points in mind, subject of course to the specific roles of the jurisdiction you are in.

If the court makes a definite ruling on the admissibility of the expert, you have properly preserved error in the pretrial hearing.

If the court makes a tentative ruling only and does not either admit or exclude the evidence, the ruling is like a ruling on a motion *in limine*. To preserve error, you must offer the evidence at trial and make objections on the record.

If the court makes a tentative ruling that the expert will be excluded, you should approach the bench at trial and, out of the hearing of the jury but within the presence of the court reporter, formally offer the expert. If the court excludes the expert, you should make an offer of proof.

If the evidence was fully developed at the pretrial hearing, you may offer the transcript of the hearing as the offer of proof. The offer should include evidence relating to the qualifications of the expert, the opinion the expert would give if permitted to testify at trial, evidence of the relevance and reliability of the opinion, and a statement of how the exclusion of the expert's opinion affected a substantial right of your client.

If the court makes a tentative ruling that your expert would be admitted, you should offer the expert during trial. The party who opposes the expert will likely object when the expert is offered and refer to the pretrial hearing in support of its objection.

The court's ruling or an expert's qualifications will be reviewed by the appellate court for abuse of discretion. The trial court has broad discretion to determine if an expert's qualifications are sufficient. The court of appeals will typically review de novo the applicability of the reliability factors to the trial court's evaluation of expert testimony.

Objecting to Experts 8

JUST AS *DAUBERT* AND ITS PROGENY opened up the possibility of allowing expert testimony that has not reached the general acceptance stage, it also required the court to exercise a healthy skepticism toward the expert and the methodology employed. An expert's opinion must be shown to be sufficiently reliable, and the purpose of the reliability analysis is to ensure that the expert uses the same level of intellectual rigor as other experts in the same field.

Most evidentiary rules, including the federal rules, require that the expert's testimony be based on sufficient facts or data, that the expert's testimony be the product of reliable principles and methods, and that the expert apply these principles and methods reliably to the facts of the case. In spite of the increasingly liberal admission of expert testimony, the courts must still perform the gatekeeping function required by the evidentiary rules.

We will discuss in later chapters the techniques for discovering information that disqualifies or discredits the witness—the deposition (Chapter 9) and the cross-examination (Chapter 11).

The Court's Role

The trial judge must determine that the expert's testimony has a reliable basis in the knowledge and experience of the discipline under consideration and that the testimony is relevant to the facts at hand. While the courts have broad discretion and flexibility in the application of this gatekeeping function, expert testimony must be carefully examined for both relevance and reliability.

Because the courts possess such broad discretion, the outcome of many cases will depend largely on the determination made by the judge in a hearing to determine the admissibility and pretrial discovery of the experts. To ensure that the expert witness who uses inadmissible evidence as the source of facts or data does not rely on unreliable sources of information, rules such as Federal Rule of Evidence 703 require that the underlying facts or data be of a type that experts in the field reasonably rely upon in the daily performance of their work.

Necessity for Experts

The initial issue is whether there is even the need to hear expert testimony. If the matter is not sufficiently complex, i.e., beyond the knowledge and experience of the ordinary layman, an expert is not necessary, and you should move the court to strike the witness on these grounds.

The area can be a complex one, but if it is one that lay people encounter routinely, the court may well determine that there is no need for expert testimony. Furthermore, if the expert's testimony does not meet a helpfulness standard similar to that expressed in Federal Rule of Evidence 702, requiring that the testimony assist the trier of fact to "understand the evidence or to determine a fact in issue," the court is obligated to exclude the evidence.

Intercepting the Testimony

When there is a dispute about the expert's opinion, such as the reasonableness of the expert's reliance on certain evidence, the trial court may resolve the issue either *in limine* or at trial. Your first goal is to intercept the testimony before the jury receives it. You may achieve this goal by resorting to Federal Rule of Evidence 104(a), which allows the trial court to make preliminary determinations as to the admissibility of testimony.

You can also voir dire the expert regarding these preliminary issues and then move to exclude the expert's testimony on the grounds that the testimony will not assist the trier of fact, that the witness is not qualified to testify as an expert, or that the expert's methodology is suspect. These preliminary determinations are within the trial court's discretion, and appellate courts will review them only upon a showing of abuse of discretion.

Examining the Expert

Once the opposing expert is identified, you should ask your consulting experts what they know about the opposing expert and, if appropriate, have them make inquiries in the relevant community. You should then attempt to obtain everything you can about the expert, especially publications that the expert has written on the subject. You should also try to review as much of the expert's prior testimony as possible. Thoroughly checking the expert's background, as well as consulting with other lawyers before whom the expert has testified, will also be helpful.

Any reports generated by the expert should be requested from opposing counsel as soon as possible. Periodic requests should be made to the expert to supplement previous interrogatory and document requests to ensure that you have the latest information.

Particular Qualifications

No matter how qualified the expert may be, those qualifications must match the particular subject matter before you. Thus, a witness may be qualified to give opinions on some matters, but not others. The expert's curriculum vitae should be thoroughly probed to determine whether there are any weaknesses, overstatements, or vulnerable areas that will allow you to question either the expert's qualifications for serving in the case or the expert's methodology in arriving at the opinions expressed.

Timing of the Objections

In deciding whether to make a challenge to your opponent's experts, it is generally true that objections arguing inadequate credentials, irrelevant discipline, or general unreliability of the methodology employed provide the greatest possibility of excluding the expert's testimony entirely. Therefore these objections should be raised as early as possible before trial.

Challenges based on inadequacy of the data employed, errors in calculations, or alternative data not considered are less likely to lead to overall exclusion. Therefore those objections may be most effectively posed on cross-examination.

Exploring the Foundation of the Opinion

At common law, an expert witness setting forth the foundation on which an opinion is based could rely only on facts or data that had been personally observed or made known to the witness at or before trial. An expert may still rely on either of those to form an opinion, but rules like Federal Rule of Evidence 703 dramatically expand the permissible bases for expert testimony and provide an additional ground on which an expert may rely:

> The facts or data in the particular case upon which an expert bases an opinion or inference may be those perceived by or made known to him at or before the hearing. *If of a type reasonably relied upon by experts in the particular field in forming opinions or inferences upon the subject the facts or data need not be admissible in evidence in order for the opinion or inference to be admitted.* (Emphasis added.)

This rule allows an expert to rely on any basis, otherwise admissible into evidence or not, as long as other experts in the field would reasonably rely upon it.

It is your role to reveal any deficiencies or inaccuracies in the underlying facts and data. Look especially for a methodology by which a conclusion may have been prematurely reached or where thoroughness may have been lacking in considering all the facts.

Disclosure of Underlying Facts

Rule 705 abandoned the requirement that an expert disclose facts underlying the opinion as a prerequisite to admissibility of the opinion itself. The object of the rule was not to eliminate questions about the foundations of the opinion. Instead, the rule contemplates that the underlying foundation for the expert's opinion will be elicited on cross-examination, especially since the federal rules permit extensive discovery of an expert's opinions and the basis for those opinions.

Problems of Eliminating Hypotheticals

The abolishment of mandating strict hypothetical questions on direct examination (as promulgated in Federal Rule of Evidence 705) does present some problems for cross-examination. The common-law procedure allowed you the opportunity to object to potentially inadmissible testimony, but now you must either second-guess opinions based on unreliable information or wait until cross-examination to discredit the inadmissible testimony.

The federal rules do not forbid the use of the hypothetical question as a means of eliciting the expert's opinion, and in most personal injury litigation the hypothetical question remains an important and useful device by which counsel can summarize the facts of the case in advance of closing argument.

Of course, the court can require you to put a confusing or prejudicial hypothetical question into more useful form. And the court can always invoke a rule like Federal Rule of Evidence 403, which provides that even relevant evidence can be excluded when it carries a danger of prejudice, confusion, or waste of time that substantially outweighs its probative value.

▼▼▼▼▼

The Role of Cross-Examination

"Vigorous cross-examination, presentation of contract evidence, and careful instruction on the burden of proof are the traditional and appropriate means of attacking shaky but admissible evidence."

Daubert, 509 U.S. at 596.

Moving to Exclude Your Opponent's Witness

Objections to expert testimony are made in three ways: (1) by motion *in limine* before trial, (2) by objection based on voir dire, if requested and granted by the court, or (3) by objection when the particular opinion is called for during testimony.

The motion *in limine* is appropriate when the court can judge from the deposition record or other evidence whether the expert testimony meets the criteria of reliability and relevance. Voir dire and objection make sense if additional facts need to be developed to demonstrate to the judge that the testimony should not be admitted.

As movant you should request a hearing on the motion. Though a hearing may not be necessary to preserve error, failure to request a pretrial ruling may result in waiver of the challenge on appeal. You should allege that there is good reason for questioning the expert's reliability and that gatekeeper proceedings (special briefing, hearings, and so forth) are necessary.

Should the request for a motion *in limine* be denied, an alternative is to ask for a voir dire examination of the expert witness outside the presence of the jury. Such a tactic will often uncover inadmissible and damaging segments of the expert's presentation.

To object to an expert's opinion, you should file a pretrial motion to exclude the expert. The motion can challenge the expert's qualifications as well as the reliability and relevance of the expert's opinion. If you seek to exclude expert testimony because the expert is not qualified, you should show that the expert does not possess the requisite higher degree of knowledge, skill, experience, training, or education. If you seek to exclude the testimony because the expert's opinions are not reliable or relevant, you must do so pursuant to the standards set forth in the appropriate evidentiary rules and supporting case law.

Factors of Reliability

In interpreting the reliability requirement, you should look to the factors developed by the courts in determining whether an expert's opinions are sufficiently reliable, beginning with the *Daubert* factors themselves. In *Kumho Tire,* the Supreme Court noted that while these factors should be considered when they are reasonable measures of reliability, they are not exclusive.

There are many factors a court may consider when evaluating reliability:

- ◆ Whether the theory or technique underlying the expert's testimony can be or has been tested.
- ◆ If appropriate, the known or potential rate of error of the technique and the existence and maintenance of standards controlling the technique's operation.
- ◆ Whether the theory or technique has been subjected to peer review and publication.
- ◆ Whether the expert's theory or technique enjoys "general acceptance" within the relevant scientific community.
- ◆ Whether the expert's testimony is based on sufficient facts or data.
- ◆ Whether the expert's opinion was developed expressly for the purpose of testifying or as a result of independent research.
- ◆ Whether the expert has unjustifiably extrapolated from an accepted premise to an unfounded conclusion.
- ◆ Whether the expert has adequately accounted for alternative explanations.
- ◆ Whether the field of expertise claimed by the expert is known to reach reliable results for the type of opinion the expert would give.

- Any other factors appropriate to ensure that the expert employs in the courtroom the same level of intellectual rigor that characterizes the practice in the relevant field.

Assisting the Trier of Fact

Most rules of evidence, like Federal Rule of Evidence 702, require that the expert's opinion assist the trier of fact in understanding the evidence or determining a fact in issue. In other words, the opinion must be relevant to the facts at issue. The party seeking to exclude expert testimony can always attempt to show that the expert's opinion will not assist the trier of fact in understanding the evidence or in determining a fact in issue. The motion should argue that the evidence supporting the expert's opinion is simply not sufficient to allow a reasonable juror to conclude that the proposition is more likely to be true than not.

Depositions of Experts

9

DEPOSITIONS OF EXPERTS ARE similar to depositions of fact witnesses only in form. In substance, the two can be miles apart. Generally speaking, the fact witness is testifying about what was observed. The expert witness is expressing a professional opinion based on knowledge and experience.

Deposing Your Opponent's Expert

The deposition of an expert witness is critical for you to determine exactly what opinions the expert holds and the methodology used to arrive at those opinions. It is also important as a potential tool to disqualify the expert for inadequate qualifications or unreliable opinions.

Considerable discovery typically will have occurred by the time you depose the expert, which allows you to plumb the depths of the expert's background, opinions, and basis for those opinions long before you take the deposition. Your thoroughness in preparing interrogatories and document requests will pay off handsomely when the time finally arrives to depose the witness.

Preparing to Take a Deposition

Preparation for the deposition of the opponent's expert should begin months in advance. Once the expert is identified by your adversary, you should attempt to obtain everything the expert has written on the subject on which testimony will be given. You should also try to obtain and review the expert's prior testimony in depositions and the courtroom in order to be familiar with the expert's previously stated opinions. A thorough check of the expert's background, as well as consultations with other lawyers for whom and against whom the expert has previously testified, is of course helpful.

One point that should not be overlooked is whether the expert's research has been funded by any particular organizations. If the expert's findings are consistent with the viewpoint of the funding organization, this information could be very useful in discrediting the witness.

The Essential Questions

Before asking the expert the basis for this opinion—the what, why, how, and when—make sure you have a complete list of all the opinions the expert has reached in your case. With this list in hand, you can then query the expert about the details of each opinion.

You should never assume that you know what the witness will say in a deposition. Start broadly and narrow the areas covered only as you gather evidence that the excluded areas are not relevant. It is critical to ask questions that reveal exactly how the expert narrowed the field of inquiry.

In general, the opposing expert should be asked:

- What opinions have been reached and what methodology was used.
- What assumptions were made in reaching those opinions.
- What tasks were not performed in the course of the expert's work.
- Who the reliable authorities in the field are.

The expert's basis for claiming that *Daubert* and other gatekeeping criteria have been met should be explored in detail at the deposition. If the expert can be forced to admit that some of the important criteria have not been satisfied, the court is more likely to exclude the opinion.

You should ask the expert about other experts who agree with him, because there may be materials that they have written that disagree with (or at least limit) the approach the testifying expert has taken. Ask whether their work is considered to be reliable. Then have your own expert review the works of these recommended experts in relevant areas to find materials to be used in the deposition.

Never forget that the opposing expert may be able to educate you in important areas. Rather than showing how much you know, let the expert assume the position of teacher. The expert may reveal information that the lawyer would prefer left unstated until trial. Additionally, you will not show your own hand too soon.

Be sure to ask the expert about the well-known authorities in the field. If the expert is reluctant to do so, challenge his or her knowledge in this area.

If the deposition reveals inadequacy of credentials, irrelevance of the particular discipline, or general unreliability of the methodology employed, these issues should be raised with the court as soon as possible, in order to exclude the expert's testimony.

Reliability Issues

To determine the reliability of opinions held by the expert being deposed, you should ask the questions like the following:

- ◆ Has the methodology appeared in a peer-reviewed publication?
- ◆ What is the error rate attributable to this methodology— and is it known or knowable?
- ◆ Has the methodology achieved general acceptance in the relevant scientific field?
- ◆ Is this methodology testable when used for these purposes—that is, are the results replicable?
- ◆ Was this methodology created for the purposes of this litigation?

Other courts have added additional criteria to this list (as encouraged to do by the *Daubert* and *Kumho Tire* decisions), and you should ask those as well. These factors do not guarantee admissibility, nor does their absence foreclose it.

Other criteria may also preclude the expert—such as the qualitative sufficiency of the data employed, the consistency of the general methodology, and the ability of the expert to articulate a clear and logical relationship between the methodology and the resulting opinion.

You should ask the expert if he used assistants to assess the information that forms the basis of the opinion. Some of these assistants may have made important decisions affecting the expert's work, and it may be worthwhile to take their depositions too.

You should ask the expert for the names of experts who disagree with his or her position and the basis for the disagreements.

Widening the Web

Your job is to extract as much information from the expert as possible, using a number of means. Ask the expert:

- ◆ About the extent of his or her knowledge concerning the particular situation that gave rise to this lawsuit. One of your biggest problems is discovering the technical aspects of the case, and the expert may be able to teach you.
- ◆ Numerous "why" questions, so that you will not only gain knowledge but learn about the expert's thought processes and theories. During trial, you would never ask such questions for fear of allowing the expert to make a speech that could damage or destroy your case.
- ◆ Broad questions, like "Tell us everything you know about. . ." The hope is that the expert may divulge too much.
- ◆ Numerous hypothetical questions in which the expert must assume certain facts. You may in the process trap the expert into testifying for your side.
- ◆ To admit that certain treatises are "authoritative" so that they can be introduced into evidence as the standard to be legally applied.

Pointing Out Omissions

One dilemma is whether to point out in the deposition the *lack* of evidence necessary to meet *Daubert* or other standards of reliability. If the parties are allowed to supplement testimony with an affidavit, it is probably a better strategy to ask witnesses about gaps in their testimony before they have a chance to talk to their counsel.

If a supplement of testimony is not allowed, your silence on the subject may be appropriate. You can then raise the issue at trial. However, some jurisdictions require you to raise *Daubert* objections before trial in order to preserve them for appeal. Knowledge of the local rules is critical in this regard.

Preparing Your Expert for Deposition

Now the shoe is on the other foot, and it is your witness that is being deposed. Experts should understand why their depositions are being taken. This is particularly important with experts without much trial experience.

You should explain to your expert that, first of all, the opposing lawyer wants to learn as much about the subject matter as possible. You should clarify that it is only necessary to answer the questions truthfully. While you want your expert to educate the jury at trial, it is not necessary to educate the opposing lawyer at the deposition.

Second, the opposing lawyer wants to know as much as possible about your expert's opinions. The expert must testify accurately regarding those opinions the opposing lawyer raises, but need not discuss opinions not inquired about or go into more detail than specifically requested.

Third, the opposing lawyer wants to pin your expert down as much as possible. Explain to the expert that it is a legitimate goal on the lawyer's part, but that it is generally to the expert's disadvantage to be too restricted.

Effective lawyers can use demeanor to disarm, agitate, or influence an expert. It will be helpful for your expert to know some of the styles used:

Charming approach. Opposing counsel attempts to disarm the witness with friendliness and therefore make the expert as relaxed as possible.

Ignorance approach. Opposing counsel pretends to know very little about the subject matter to encourage your expert to answer at length and volunteer information.

Aggressive approach. Opposing counsel attempts to intimidate or agitate your expert in order to get him or her to misspeak.

Your expert should also know that opposing counsel may change from one demeanor to another during the deposition—ignorant to induce the expert to go into too much detail, friendly to establish a calm and nonthreatening atmosphere, and then aggressive to pin down the expert.

The Expert's File

Because the expert's file may be subject to review and examination by opposing counsel, you should go through the entire file so you are not caught by surprise in the middle of the deposition. It could be very damaging if the expert has notes that indicate problem areas or what you would like to accomplish from the testimony.

Usually there is no need for the expert to retain notes of inspections or preliminary calculations. If asked by opposing counsel if the file contains everything generated in the investigation and analysis of the case, your expert can explain that it did not seem necessary to save every piece of paper, and that all materials are reflected in the expert report.

Unless specifically requested by opposing counsel, experts should not have copies of their invoices in the file. They can explain that billing is kept in a separate file and they do not know the exact amount of charges or the amount of time spent on the project.

▼▼▼▼▼

Practice Pointer

You should seek a protective order to prevent disclosure of the work the witness is doing for other clients, since such information is useful to the opposing counsel in determining the consistency of the expert's work.

Explaining Applicable Law

It is not necessary that your expert have an in-depth understanding of the law, but the expert should be at least familiar with the basic substantive law involved in the case. There are certain words and phrases that have a particular meaning in the law, such as "unreasonably dangerous," "defect," and "standard of care." Sometimes a particular word has a different meaning in medicine or engineering than in the law. You should discuss these important terms so that the expert understands the significance of key words.

The expert should also understand the evidentiary matters that may affect his or her testimony. The expert must realize that an opinion is to be based on a reasonable degree of medical, scientific, or engineering certainty. Emphasis of the word "certainty" should convince an expert to refrain from offering an unsupportive opinion.

Reviewing Factual Basis

One of the most important aspects of predeposition preparation is a review of the factual basis for the expert's opinions. The expert must know which facts are in dispute and which are not. Remember, if the jury resolves a disputed underlying fact against you, it could undermine some or all of your expert's opinions. In most jurisdictions, including the federal courts, your expert can present otherwise inadmissible evidence before a jury by stating that the facts or data typically are relied on by experts in the particular discipline.

Providing Appropriate Responses

While the scope of questioning by an opposing lawyer can be as varied as a fertile mind can conceive, there are areas of questioning that typically recur at experts' depositions. Your expert should be made aware of these areas and be able to give appropriate responses.

▼▼▼▼▼

Common Deposition Advice

Common pointers given to witnesses to heed during the deposition include the following:

◆ Do not answer a question until you understand it. If the question is unclear, ask the lawyer to repeat it or phrase it in clearer language.

◆ Think about each question before answering it. Do not supply information not requested by the question, even though you may think it is relevant. If the lawyer does not ask you all you know, do not volunteer information.

◆ If you do not know the answer to a question, simply say, "I do not know." Do not feel that just because a question is asked, you are expected to know the answer. Do not guess or assume.

◆ Give factual information only if you have firsthand knowledge of the facts. Do not base your answer on hearsay information, unless you are specifically asked to do so.

◆ If asked, do not hide any facts you are personally aware of, unless you are instructed by your counsel not to answer.

◆ If a question of fact is asked, make it a practice to check it against any records you may have. This is a prudent practice even if you are sure of the answer.

◆ Do not look for traps in every question. There are not many trick questions, and if one comes along your counsel will object to it. Do not try to second-guess each question or you will create the appearance of calculation, apprehension, or indecision.

◆ You can be required to give a simple yes or no answer to a proper question. If, however, the lawyer cuts you off in the middle of an important explanation, you should state that you have not finished your answer.

◆ If an objection is made by your counsel, stop speaking immediately. If your counsel advises or instructs you not to answer the question, do not answer.

◆ Do not argue with opposing counsel, and never become angry or hostile. Remain calm and unemotional, even if the lawyer is acting outrageously.

◆ You must fight against showing any exasperation, boredom, or fatigue.

◆ Do not be afraid to admit that you have had conferences with your lawyer. If the opposing counsel asks you, "Did your counsel tell you what to say at this deposition?" you should simply answer "My lawyer told me to tell the truth."

Unknown Answers   The best answer for an expert who does not know the answer to a question is, "I don't know." The answer "I don't remember" is perfectly acceptable when the witness does not remember. Speculation by the witness invites uncertainty and the serious possibility of error. And the response "I don't understand the question" is certainly appropriate when the question is vague or ambiguous. Let the questioner select a better question rather than having the witness assist in formulating the proper question. If the witness is uncertain about what to do, he should ask for a break to consult with you.

Information Considered   The expert must be the one who decides which information to consider and which to ignore. In response to the question asking who selected the information considered, the expert must be able to truthfully say, "I did." Otherwise, the credibility of the witness is severely compromised.

Restrictive Questions   It is the desire of every lawyer to pin a witness down so tightly that testimony can be severely restricted. The process often will start with a series of seemingly obvious questions in which words such as "all," "none," "every," "always," and "never" are used to lock in the expert. Those words should alert the expert to impending trouble. Often the best response is: "It's difficult to say 'all,' but that is everything that comes to mind at this moment."

Opposing counsel will also want to pin down the bases of the expert's opinion. When referring to the sources or treatises on which the expert relies, it is acceptable to mention a few, but your expert must explain that opinions or conclusions are a mélange of data learned and observed.

Your expert may thus rely on a composite of formal education, continuing education, books, journals, experience, and various informal sources for his or her opinions and conclusions. The following response is therefore appropriate: "My opinions are based on accumulated knowledge from years of study and analysis in this area. It is not possible to describe everything that has contributed to my knowledge of this subject."

Completed Analysis   The opposing lawyer will no doubt want to elicit a commitment from your expert that the analysis of the case is complete. That may not be appropriate because additional information may yet to be developed through discovery or other sources. A good response is: "As with any study, there is an ongoing process. Additional facts may be developed or scientific knowledge discovered. If that occurs, I believe it would only further support my opinions. But my analysis is always ongoing."

Learned Treatises   Prepare the expert for attempts to lay foundation for "learned treatises." Under federal rules, if a work is established as a reliable authority by the testimony of the opposing expert witness, relevant portions may be read into the record as substantive evidence and as an exception to the hearsay rule. When confronted with a request at a deposition to identify reliable authorities, the best response is along the lines of, "There are several good works out there. But I would have to know exactly what you are interested in to determine whether a particular treatise is reliable on that point."

Recognized Authorities   Many lawyers will attempt to get an opposing expert to admit that their expert is a "recognized authority." Don't let your expert acknowledge the opposing expert as a "recognized authority." Rather, your expert can respond, "Dr.

Doe, like many engineers, has published in this area. But I don't know that she is any more knowledgeable than the others."

Likewise, many lawyers would like to get your expert to admit that a specific book or treatise is "authoritative." Your expert must be cautioned that the opponent will find something in that publication to challenge your expert's opinions. Therefore, your expert should avoid acknowledging a publication as such, responding thus: "As with most published works, the author makes statements with which I agree and others with which I may disagree."

If the opposing counsel presses the subject, your expert can respond: "If you would like me to comment on a specific portion of the text, please ask me about that."

Inaccurate Attribution Sometimes the opposing lawyer will misquote your expert's prior testimony, either intentionally or not. In this situation your expert should immediately correct the lawyer in a polite but firm manner. Sometimes opposing counsel will attempt to summarize the expert's testimony, but do so incompletely or erroneously. If this happens, your expert should respond: "I am sorry, you must have misunderstood me. I certainly did not say what you just described."

Time Spent on Case Often the opposing lawyer will try to get a commitment from your expert about the amount of time spent in reviewing and analyzing the case. They may even refer to a billing statement indicating the amount of hours charged by the expert. Your expert should respond that he is not sure how much time he has spent so far. If the opposing lawyer presses the issue further, your expert can respond: "I have spent enough time to be absolutely sure of my opinions."

Fees Charged An opposing lawyer usually will ask about fees. The expert should make it clear that he has been paid for the time spent in analyzing the case and testifying, but that he is not being paid to testify in a certain manner. It is also helpful if the expert can state that the fees he has charged are the ones he customarily charges for such work.

▼▼▼▼▼

Cautionary Answers

Your expert should be warned to be especially cautious about questions that

♦ Focus on documents, records, and facts provided to the expert for review.

♦ Deal with information the expert conveyed to the client or counsel, because it may solicit privileged information.

♦ Ask "why," because such questions not only gain knowledge but indicate your thought processes and theories.

♦ Start with "Tell us everything you can about. . . ."

♦ Concern hypothetical situations that attempt to trap you into becoming an expert witness for the other side.

♦ Ask the expert to admit that a treatise or article is "authoritative."

Follow-Up Questions

Prepare the expert to be able to make an affirmative statement of opinion in your own follow-up questioning, so that this testimony can perhaps be used later in a motion for summary judgment. The expert should also be advised to feel free to express concerns that her opinions have not been fairly portrayed or were excluded from the record by procedural ploys of opposing counsel.

Direct Examination of Experts | **10**

DIRECT EXAMINATION CAN AND SHOULD be just as impressive to the jury as an effective cross-examination. To keep the jury's interest you should move directly to the main issues and emphasize the expert's most relevant qualifications. All questions about the expert's opinions should be predicated on review of specified materials, and the expert's experience and expertise should be indicated when appropriate.

The expert's conclusions must be convincingly explained, and the bases for those conclusions provided in a clear and easily understood manner. If possible, charts, graphs, slides, and other demonstrative aids should be used to make the presentation more interesting. It is especially helpful if at the end of the testimony, a summarizing graphic of some kind can be used to remind the jury of the expert's conclusions.

The Underlying Theme

The direct examination of the expert should, of course, have as its main purpose the persuasion of the fact finder to your client's position in the litigation. But behind that goal you should always have in mind the evidentiary requirements for the testimony of the specific expert before you, as set forth, for example, in Federal Rule of Evidence 702:

> If scientific, technical, or other specialized knowledge will assist the trier of fact to understand the evidence or to determine a fact in issue, a witness qualified as an expert by knowledge, skill, experience, training, or education, may testify thereto in the form of an opinion or otherwise, if (1) the testimony is based upon sufficient facts or data, (2) the testimony is the product of reliable principles and methods, and (3) the witness has applied the principles and methods reliably to the facts of the case.

Essentially, subpart (1) requires that experts have adequate reason for reaching the opinions about which they propose to testify. For scientific testimony, this might include confirming that the expert possesses adequate knowledge in the particular field or has conducted research in the area. For nonscientific testimony, you should demonstrate that the expert has enough experience with or sufficient study of the subject at hand.

Subpart (2) requires that the expert reach his conclusion from the facts or data scrutinized. Even if the expert has adequate knowledge of or experience with the subject of his testimony, he must also employ a reliable methodology to reach his conclusion.

And subpart (3) requires that the expert's conclusions themselves are a reasonable result of the process and supporting facts.

Foundational Aspects of the Opinion

Federal Rule of Evidence 703 and its state equivalents allow an expert to rely on any basis, otherwise admissible into evidence or not, as long as other experts in the field would "reasonably" rely on it. The purpose of Rule 703's broadening of the permissible basis of expert opinion testimony is to bring the practice of the courts in line with that of the experts themselves in their everyday lives. Much information that experts routinely rely on should be admissible as evidence, even though the foundation itself may be difficult or time-consuming to prove. This rule relieves the parties of the difficult, if not impossible, burden of parading a string of witnesses into court to do nothing more than authenticate documents confirming evidence on which other experts have reasonably and routinely relied.

Role of the Examiner

The role of the direct examiner has also been made considerably easier by evidentiary rules eliminating the requirement that the lawyer elicit from the expert all the facts underlying the expert's opinion. The burden is now instead on the cross-examiner to expose the problems and contradictions in the opposing expert's opinion.

Evidentiary rules like Federal Rule 705 govern the foundational questioning of expert witnesses at trial. The rule departs from the common law by permitting an expert to give opinion testimony without first testifying to the facts or data underlying the opinion. The rule also does not require any particular form of questioning, such as hypotheticals.

However, the court still retains its discretion to require disclosure of underlying facts or data, or the use of certain types of questioning, if it finds it necessary to do so.

The object of Rule 705 is not to eliminate foundational questioning entirely, but to ensure that questions in the direct examination move along as briskly as possible. The necessity for orderly presentation often leads to divulgence of at least some of this supporting material anyway.

Preparing Your Expert for Direct

Expert witnesses must realize that although favorable testimony is desirable, they must not assume the role of an advocate. Testimony with a strong bias quickly loses its effectiveness and is vulnerable to a devastating cross-examination.

In the beginning it is important to emphasize whatever differences exist between your expert and your opponents and, if so, to render those into qualifications. Any differences in credentials, approach, and style between your expert and your opponent's expert should be emphasized. If your expert has chosen a methodology that the other expert did not, then highlight that. Make certain that your expert is animated, uses interesting graphical aids, and speaks in terms understandable to the ordinary person.

Substance of Testimony

To prepare your expert for direct examination, a few points should be kept in mind.

- You should make the expert familiar enough with your plan of interrogation to know what topics will be covered, what facts will be established, and what signals you will use to switch topics or control the direction of testimony.
- The expert should be questioned in a mock situation in the same style that you will use in court. The questions should also be arranged in generally the same order that they will be presented at trial, but use different wording at trial so that the exchange will appear spontaneous.
- The expert must be able to explain and define any technical terms she will use in court. These definitions must be consistent with technical dictionaries and other reference materials.
- You should review the expert's theories in detail and challenge them aggressively. The expert's theories should not only be viable, but must impress the judge and jury with their sincerity and common sense.
- You should prepare the expert to handle questions relating to his or her qualifications as an expert.
- You should indicate to the expert how much detail is necessary in his or her responses.
- Any real or demonstrative evidence should be thoroughly reviewed, as well as any questions you may use to properly authenticate it.

Style of Delivery

The expert must communicate effectively with the judge and jury. A few tips on style are in order. The expert should:

- Appear comfortable, not stilted, on the stand.
- Be careful not to patronize.

- Speak in a straightforward manner using clear and simple terms.
- Strive to be positive and assertive, but not arrogant.
- Maintain a professional demeanor without nervous mannerisms.
- Dress neatly and in accordance with the seriousness of the occasion.
- Speak directly to the judge and jury and loudly enough that they can hear.

Admission of Qualifications

Prepare your expert to summarize his or her strongest qualifications and to emphasize the connection between those credentials and the work completed in the case. The judge or jury can then see the relevance of the witness's education, training, and experience to the issue at hand. In other words, the credentials of the expert can be seen as demonstrating the helpfulness of the witness, as required by the evidentiary rules of most jurisdictions.

Direct Examination of Your Expert

Proving Qualifications

There are two primary strategies for proving the qualifications of your expert—the traditional approach and the cumulative approach.

Traditional Approach   The traditional approach is simply to elicit testimony describing every diploma, certificate, license, publication, professional membership, and qualifying experience the expert has ever acquired. This initial citing of all the expert's qualifications is the safest approach and should normally be used if a realistic chance for challenging the expert's qualifications exists.

When you choose the traditional strategy or it is required by the court, it is within the court's discretion to allow you to read the *curriculum vitae* and then merely ask the expert if those are the relevant qualifications. The danger of this technique is that the jury's attention will wander. Jurors can easily forget the specific qualifications that underlie the expert's opinions and conclusions.

▼▼▼▼▼

Practice Pointer

After reading the details of the expert's educational background, ask "Does that accurately summarize your educational background and qualifications?" After the witness answers "Yes," you can proceed with a statement such as, "Let's now go to your practical on-the-job experience."

Then read the expert's occupational history, including duties and responsibilities at each position, and again conclude with a question such as, "Does the list just read accurately summarize your professional work-related experiences?"

You can then continue in this manner through the various categories of experiences on which the expert's qualifications are based. The interaction from the witness after each category of experience helps break up the monotony of reading the entire *curriculum vitae.*

The other advantage of this approach is that you enhance the impact of the expert's testimony by establishing that the expert is qualified to provide opinions on a specific subject.

Cumulative Approach The cumulative approach provides an initial overview of the expert's qualifications and then fills in additional details as the testimony progresses toward the main issues. Trial judges and jurors appreciate this effort to save time and provide interest. Some of the monotony of reading a resume can be alleviated by dividing the expert's qualification into categories and eliciting some interaction from the witness after reading each one.

The strategy of the cumulative approach is to avoid a long, drawn-out rendition of every detail of the expert's qualifications, and instead to introduce evidence before inquiring about the expert's particular opinion. This strategy is more convincing because the expert's qualifications on a specific matter are established immediately prior to the particular opinion on that subject.

Stipulation of Expert's Qualifications Driven by the urge to save time, lawyers are sometimes tempted to stipulate that the opposing expert is qualified. But it is rare for opposing counsel to accept such a stipulation because the more the jury hears about the expert's qualifications, the more weight they accord the testimony.

You must be prepared to counter this "timesaving" ploy. Consider responding, "While I appreciate counsel's acknowledgement of the expertise of my expert, I sincerely feel that the jury needs to understand my expert's qualifications in order to properly assess the credibility of his conclusions. But aware of the importance of saving time, I will be brief."

A summary of the expert's major qualifications can then be read to the jury in place of the usual questions and answers about each entry on the *curriculum vita*. Then you can elicit brief witness interaction following the reading of each category of the witness's qualifications.

Striving for Brevity

Typically, the best strategy for direct examination is to get to the point quickly. After establishing the expert's qualifications, you should immediately follow with a question as to why the expert was retained.

Q: Dr. Smith, do you consider yourself to be an expert in pathology?

A: That's correct.

Q: We're going to ask your opinions in this case. Will you give us your opinions in reasonable medical probability.

A: Certainly.

Q: Before we get to your opinions, I'd like to talk to you briefly about your education and training. You have provided us with a copy of your current CV, have you not?

Strive for brevity, clarity, and speed without omitting anything necessary to fully explain the basis of the expert's opinion. Brevity is essential because your expert should have impact, and you do not want to detract from that impact by providing too many details. Overkill can bore jurors and open up subjects that otherwise would not be available for cross-examination. Moreover, some of the details underlying your expert's opinions will be more impressive when provided in response to questions on cross-examination.

By maintaining control and interjecting the opinion question, you will be less likely to raise an objection that you are leading the witness. Furthermore, the follow-up question will make the question-and-answer sequence seem less rehearsed.

Exuding Modesty

A little modesty from the expert in describing qualifications goes a long way with the jury:

> Q: Are you an expert on clots?
> A: Since it's a little arrogant to sit here and say one is an expert, let's talk about what I mean by expert. I mean someone with special experience and knowledge.
>
> As I have pointed out, I was part of the clinical trials that led to government approval of clot busters. In that sense, I am an expert.
>
> If you're talking about someone that works in a laboratory and works with test tubes and Petri dishes, I certainly am not.

Educating the Jury

One of the greatest contributions of an expert is the ability to educate the jury. The more clarity one brings to the issue the more persuasive one becomes:

> Q: Could you tell the jury, please: What is pathology?
> A: Pathology is the study of disease. It is usually divided into two broad categories. There is anatomic pathology, which includes autopsy pathology and surgical pathology. And then there is cytopathology, which is the study of cellular detail.
> Q: Is it possible to see the actual slides of Mr. Holder's coronary arteries?
> A: Yes.
> Q: Do we have a microscope in the courtroom to help us do that?
> A: We do.
> Q: Looking at these slides, please tell us what we're looking at.

When dealing with complex subjects, analogy is an important aspect of this education process.

Q: Describe what a blood clot is made of.

A: Basically there are two things that make the blood clot. The platelets are the individual particles and would be like bricks in a brick wall. The liquid part of the blood that clots consists of chemicals that come together to form a mesh. That would be like the mortar between the bricks. It starts out very liquid, but starts to seal up and become a sold mortar called fibrin.

The Expert's Opinion

At last one comes to the heart of the expert's opinion. You should first ask the expert if he or she has an opinion, and when the expert replies in the affirmative, you should ask what the opinion is:

Q: Based on your training, your experience, your research, and your review of the records in this case, do you have an opinion as to the cause of Mr. Silversmith's death?

A: I do.

Q: What is that?

A: I think that within reasonable medical probability that he died of ventricular fibrillation. That rhythm was actually seen by EMS at the scene. And that was due to his severe underlying coronary artery disease, which has been well described in the pathology. He had mild to severe coronary arteriosclerosis in two arteries, including the artery of death. He probably had underlying ischemia as evidenced by the fibrosis at the autopsy, and this ischemia triggered the life-threatening arrhythmia.

Q: Have you seen examples of this type of death in your career?

A: See it all the time. Unfortunately, we see it with people who know they have underlying coronary disease, and they suffer ischemia and die suddenly. And we certainly see it in patients with unsuspected severe arteriosclerosis.

Under Federal Rule of Evidence 703 and its counterparts at the state level, an expert may rely on facts or data perceived or made known to the expert before the hearing. Moreover, the expert may rely on inadmissible facts or data as long as they are of a type reasonably relied on in forming opinions or inferences by experts in the field.

The effect of the rule, however, goes beyond documentary evidence. It allows experts to base their opinions on, for example, the results of unreported experiments that they have learned about by conferring with other experts. Trial courts retain much discretion in this area, but they often defer to the experts' judgment regarding the reliability of the sources on which they base their opinions.

Under this rule, out-of-court statements otherwise excluded as hearsay may be received as evidence for the purpose of demonstrating the basis of the expert's opinion. The trend to broaden the scope of the facts and data that experts may rely on has eliminated many technical objections during trial.

You can more easily corroborate your experts' opinions by producing both published and privately circulated documentary evidence establishing that your experts' opinions are shared by eminent practitioners in the field. Because of this rule (and the hearsay exception for learned treatises), experts should search the technical literature for corroborating evidence for their testimony.

What the Expert Reviewed

It is helpful to summarize on direct examination all the sources of information that your expert reviewed before arriving at his opinion. It also shows that the expert is conscientious and has arrived at a decision only after much consideration and effort:

> Q: Now let's talk about the specific materials that you reviewed in this case. Have you reviewed all the records that were available on Mr. Cobb?
>
> A: I reviewed all the records I was given. I assume they're all that's available.
>
> Q: Did you review the autopsy report?
>
> A: I did.
>
> Q: Did you review the records from the medical examiner's office?
>
> A: I did.
>
> Q: Did you review the EMT records?
>
> A: Yes, I did.
>
> Q: Did you review the deposition of Mrs. Cobb?

A: I did.

Q: Did you review Dr. Lancaster's testimony?

A: Yes.

Q: Did you review Dr. Bronner's testimony?

A: Yes.

Q: Based on your review of the available medical records, tell us what you can about Mr. Cobb and his medical history.

Using Hypothetical Questions

Despite the trend toward broadening the scope of the data on which expert opinion can be based, some jurisdictions continue to hold that the basis must be either personal knowledge or facts contained in a hypothetical question. The general rule in these jurisdictions is that there must be sufficient facts, either already in evidence or disclosed by the witness as a result of his or her investigation, to take the testimony out of the realm of guesswork and speculation.

Hypothetical questions continue to be tactically important at trial, even in jurisdictions (such as the federal courts) that no longer require them. The hypothetical question provides an opportunity to effectively summarize and argue to the jury the facts supporting your theory of recovery. The law generally requires that there be facts in evidence sufficient to support the assumptions on which the hypothetical question is based. A hypothetical question should not assume any facts not in evidence unless reasonable assurance has been provided that such facts will be produced later in the proceedings.

The facts assumed in the hypothetical, however, need not be undisputed. It is permissible for you to assume a state of facts that you contend is justified by the evidence and that enables the witness to form an intelligent answer.

Hypothetical questions should always be prepared prior to trial based on facts gained through discovery. These facts can be supplemented at trial if additional evidence or admissions warrant it. You should have copies of the hypothetical situation available so that the trial judge, opposing counsel, and your expert witness can follow along as you recite the facts of your hypothetical.

After the witness agrees to answer a hypothetical, you should then describe the scenario of events in the clearest and most logical fashion possible with the strongest facts in evidence. To avoid objections or interruptions, you should document the proof for each fact asserted, i.e., the reference to a page in a deposition.

Each time you ask the expert to assume a certain fact established by a particular document, it should be tendered and referred to by its exhibit number. If a fact comes from deposition testimony, specifically refer to the name of the deponent, the date of the deposition, and to the page number from which the fact is taken. This provides the evidentiary foundation for each fact the expert's opinion will be based on while refreshing the jurors' memories concerning previously admitted evidence.

The assumptions on which the hypothetical question is based will be most persuasive if disputed facts are intermixed with certain undisputed facts in the case. There are always undisputed facts that can be used in formulating the hypothetical question. The goal in commingling disputed and undisputed facts is that jurors are more inclined to accept your interpretation of disputed facts when they see how those facts converge with uncontroverted facts.

Eliciting Opinion on Ultimate Issues

The law formerly prevented experts from providing opinions on ultimate issues because doing so was considered an invasion of the jury's province. That prohibition has now been removed in most jurisdictions. Federal Rule of Evidence 704 expressly states that an otherwise admissible expert opinion or inference is not objectionable because it embraces an ultimate issue to be decided by the trier of fact.

Therefore, you may want to ask your witness on direct examination a question like: "Assuming the facts I have just described, and based on your expertise and experience, do you have an opinion in reasonable scientific probability as to whether or not the design of this product was a producing cause of plaintiff's injuries?" When your expert answers yes, you should then ask, "What is that opinion?" and then of course elicit the reasons supporting that opinion.

Utilizing Prior Testimony

Showing that the expert has testified for both sides of the docket is the best way to eliminate any hint of bias:

> Q: Have you provided testimony on behalf of pharmaceutical companies in the past?
> A: I have.
> Q: Have you also provided testimony on behalf of plaintiffs in cases alleging that a pharmaceutical product was the cause of a patient's death?
> A: I have.

If you anticipate that opposing counsel will eventually emphasize the number of times that your expert has testified exclusively for plaintiffs or defendants, you should consider turning that to advantage by using it to emphasize the expert's qualifications. For example, you might say "Based on your many investigations and evaluations, have you been called on to offer your expert opinions and conclusions throughout the country?"

It is also best if you can establish that the expert's customary consultation fees are the same whether the expert is retained by plaintiffs or defendants.

One strategy to diffuse the defendant's efforts to characterize a plaintiff's expert as a "hired gun" is to elicit testimony establishing the expert's associations with defense counsel or manufacturers. It is rare for a qualified expert to have had *no* association with defense counsel or manufacturers. Most experts will have at least lectured before professional groups that included manufacturers, and most professional papers are published in journals read by members of the business community.

Even if your expert has always testified for one side of the docket, he or she has almost certainly been contacted by the other side. To use such information to your advantage, you should ask the expert if he or she has been contacted by lawyers for corporations or plaintiffs. You can then ask, "After you gave them your analysis and opinions, did they call you as an expert on their behalf?" When the witness answers no, the jury will get the message that lawyers did not like the expert's opinions even though recognizing his or her expertise.

Criticizing Expert Opinions of the Opposition

You must show that your expert is more qualified than the opponent's. This can be done tactfully:

> Q: Could you please tell the jury how your qualifications and experience differ from those of Dr. Black?
>
> A: Dr. Black is a board-certified electrophysiologist. I believe he spends the majority of his time taking care of patients and implanting defibrillators and pacemakers. He is well published.
>
>   I guess the difference is that I have spent most of my time in arrhythmia and have been involved in the major clinical trials we have been discussing. I have worked with the FDA most of my career. I feel this makes me uniquely qualified to talk about a case like this.

However, you should make clear that your expert disagrees with the conclusions of the opposing expert:

> Q: There has been testimony from Dr. Edwards that the blood clot was dislodged by CPR.
>
> A: I don't mean to be disrespectful, but that's a preposterous notion for several reasons.
>
> Q: Go ahead and explain.

Criticizing Evidence of the Opposition

Using your witness to provide a summary of how the opposing party has failed to provide adequate evidence can be devastating:

> Q: Is a heart attack something that you can just assume, or do you need evidence of it?
>
> A: The diagnosis of a heart attack is not a diagnosis of exclusion. You have to have at least some evidence.
>
> Q: Let's look at whether the plaintiffs have presented any such evidence. Let's start with the clinical. Have the plaintiffs presented any evidence that Mr. Williams had any symptoms of a heart attack?
>
> A: No.

Q: Have they presented any evidence that the enzymes showed a heart attack?

A: No.

Q: Let's look at the pathology side. Is there any evidence grossly that Mr. Williams had a heart attack?

A: No.

Q: Is there any evidence microscopically that he had a heart attack?

A: No.

Q: Is there any evidence of a clot or plaque rupture or fissure?

A: No.

Q: Is there any clinical evidence that Mr. Williams had a heart attack?

A: No.

Q: Is there any pathological evidence that he had a heart attack?

A: No.

Learned Treatises

If you seek substantive admissibility of the learned treatise, a formal offer for that purpose is necessary. Merely reading portions of the text to the expert does not make the contents of the treatise admissible for the truth of the quoted material.

Federal Rule of Evidence 803(18), for example, imposes three conditions on admissibility of the treatise on direct examination. First, the proponent must establish that the treatise or article constitutes a "reliable authority." Second, the treatise or article must be relied on by the expert giving testimony in the direct examination. Third, the relevant statements, when admitted, may be read in evidence but may not be received as exhibits.

Demonstrative Evidence

Most effective expert testimony includes some sort of demonstrative evidence that maintains the jury's interest and further cements the expert's learned opinion in their mind.

Q: Did you bring a slide to show us what the artery would look like after angioplasty?

A: Yes, I brought a slide of a patient who had angioplasty performed.

Q: Tell us, then, what we are looking at.

A: This is a coronary artery. You remember the artery comes off the aorta and supplies the heart muscle.

There's some irregularity here, which is arteriosclerosis. Then you have further blockage in this area. You can see that the artery is a lot wider here.

The point is this person has significant narrowing.

And then we go to the next picture. Several of my partners do angioplasty and stinting and they can open up the artery.

Here is the same artery opened up.

Summarizing the Evidence

Juries love summaries, and the expert should be prepared to provide them in a clear and concise manner:

Q: Could you tell us what the tests show us about any evidence of a heart attack in this case?

A: As I have summarized, a heart attack can be diagnosed by two different means—clinical and pathological. So let's go through them one by one.

Were there symptoms of a heart attack—history of chest pain, left arm pain, numbness in the chin? From my reading of Mrs. Durrett's deposition, there was no type of specific symptom that would suggest a myocardial infarction. So I think we can cross that out.

Were there EKG findings of a myocardial infarction? There were not. But, in fairness, the patient was already in ventricular fibrillation, so we didn't really have a rhythm that could have shown ST segment depression or ST segment elevation or T-wave inversions or a Q wave, some of the EKG findings of a heart attack. So it's really noninformative. So, I'm only going to put one "X" through that. We don't have evidence of it, but we don't have all the material that we would have liked to have had to be able to completely say that EKG did not show MI.

What about the enzymes? These were not drawn, so we have no enzymes in the blood to indicate there was a heart attack. But since we don't know either way, I'm not going to put an "X," I'm going to put one line through it.

What about pathology? Were there any gross changes to the naked eye? There were none. So I'm going to put an "X" on that one.

Was there microscopic evidence? The first microscopic evidence should appear about six hours after a myocardial infarction. But there wasn't any. There was no evidence that the heart muscle was dead before the patient died completely. So I'm going to put an "X" there.

Finally, was there a thrombus like I showed you in the picture? Not only was there no evidence of a clot, but there was no sign of a fissured plaque. So I can put an "X" there.

Compensation

Your expert need not be timid in admitting that he has been paid for his services:

Q: But the company has paid you for consulting, haven't they?
A: Absolutely.

Redirect

If opposing counsel cuts your expert off in the middle of an important explanation, the expert should state that he has not finished his answer so that you can ask him to amplify his answer during redirect examination.

Federal Rule 703 does not bar adverse parties from disclosing inadmissible underlying information when cross-examining experts about the basis of their opinions. And once the adverse party has opened the door, you are free to refer to it during redirect, even if the trial court initially determined that the proponent could not reveal the inadmissible evidence to the jury during the expert's direct examination.

Cross-Examination of Experts | **11**

In THE SCHEME OF expert witness testimony, the Federal Rules of Evidence have incontrovertibly placed a heightened importance on cross-examination in exploring the facts and assumptions underlying the opinion of the expert witness.

The well-known and colorful trial lawyer Gerry Spence once made an important observation about the hazards of cross-examining experts:

> There is no wealth greater than the wealth of mind filled to brimming with the facts and science of one's case. But I see the expert as a caged lion. We can get in that cage and wrestle with him if we want. But he will devour us. We can argue all day and deep into the night, and despite our superior current academic knowledge he will win the argument, because the argument seems to be, as it is, an argument between a lawyer and a scientific expert.

Mr. Spence continued with this description of the dilemma faced by the cross-examiner:

The jury has to decide who is to be believed—the lawyer who is an expert in the law, or the witness who is an expert in his science. The winner is preordained. We argue and it sounds like argument. We protest and holler and it sounds like that—and the winner, still, is the expert. There is a built-in futility in demeaning the knowledge of the expert by attempting to show our own superior freshly acquired knowledge. (*Win Your Case* [St. Martins 2005])

Conducting cross-examination without preparation is dangerous enough, but the situation is greatly exacerbated when the witness is an expert. An expert is generally a person of intelligence who is experienced in expressing ideas persuasively, and who is infinitely more knowledgeable about his or her field than you are. To make matters worse, the expert's testimony is usually given substantial weight by a jury.

There are, however, reasons why an expert can be the most vulnerable witness in a trial. First of all, jurors do not always personally relate to expert witnesses, who seem to be placed in a rarified position. And a well-prepared and motivated lawyer can often learn enough about the expert's field to counter much of the testimony.

Discovering the Expert's Reliability

The trial judge must determine that the expert testimony has a reliable basis in the knowledge and experience of the discipline under consideration and that the testimony is relevant to the facts at hand. While the courts have broad discretion and flexibility in the application of this gatekeeping function, expert testimony must be examined closely for both relevance and reliability.

Because of the flexibility of the standard articulated in *Kumho Tire,* some courts will examine the admissibility of expert testimony with greater rigor and be more willing to exclude expert testimony than the case under previous standards. Federal Rule of Evidence 702 was not designed to disqualify certain classes of expert testimony, but focused instead on the methodology of the particular expert under consideration.

Areas of expertise that were more readily admissible in the past will be subject to careful examination to ensure that the opinion espoused is based on reliable methodology. This emphasis on methodology and its application, rather than the area of expertise, is critical.

Foundational Evidence

Because the rules of evidence no longer require an explicit foundation for expert opinion, you as the cross-examiner have been elevated in position. It is the cross-examiner who must now reveal the shaky grounds on which the opposing expert's opinion relies.

Federal Rules of Evidence 703 and 705 place the burden of exploring the facts and assumptions underlying the testimony of an expert witness on opposing counsel's cross-examination. If you fail to challenge the expert testimony on cross-examination, you cannot complain about its admission.

Pretrial Preparation for Cross-Examination

You should take full advantage of all discovery—depositions, interrogatories, and your own research—to gain an even footing with the opposing expert. To effectively cross-examine an expert, you must become exceedingly familiar not only with the evidence but with the qualifications of the witness.

Begin by determining whether the expert is a bona fide expert in the field or simply a professional witness. Obtain copies of every book, article, treatise, thesis, dissertation, and speech written by the expert. Obtain transcripts from other hearings and trials where the expert has testified. Run the expert's name through the appropriate computer databases. Examine the lawsuit index in relevant areas. Check on the expert's professional status with the appropriate licensing agency.

Consultation with other experts in the field is essential for effective cross-examination. The psychological advantages of an expert witness are greatly diminished when you appear equally conversant in the area of testimony. And by using books or treatises written by the expert or his colleagues that conflict with the expert's opinion, you can erode the professional image of the expert.

Challenges Facing the Cross-Examiner

The adversary system relies heavily on the cross-examining lawyer to reveal the extent to which the expert's testimony is formed by the party hiring him. The jury has a right to know who is really testifying, and they will have to learn this during the cross-examination. You must strive to reveal mistakes made by the expert, problems with the research that underlies the expert's opinion, and flaws in the expert's application of his or her findings to the facts at hand.

Even when an opposing expert has been called to point out the scientific or other technical flaws in the expert's work, only you can point to the retaining lawyer's control of the expert as the reason for those flaws. For jurors, it is helpful to have more than the conflicting testimony of two qualified experts. If you can establish that the opposing lawyer exercised excessive control over the expert, the jurors will have evidence not only of the flaws in the analysis but the reason for those flaws. The result is devastating to the integrity of the expert.

Reasonable Degree of Certainty

The federal evidentiary rules do not require absolute certainty of expert testimony. The expert's explanatory theory, however, must satisfy the "reasonable degree of certainty" standard. Thus, you may ask the expert on cross-examination whether his or her opinion on a particular issue has a reasonable degree of scientific, medical, or other technical certainty. Although this standard is incapable of a precise definition, the standard calls for conformity with a generally accepted explanatory theory used in the field. An expert's inability to state his or her opinion with a reasonable degree of certainty will not affect its admissibility but will go to the weight of the testimony.

Basis of the Opinion

The Federal Rules of Evidence now encourage experts not only to explain evidence but to verify the source of evidence. Rule 703 seemingly approves the admission of hearsay evidence through expert testimony, and it has been characterized as a "back door exception" to the general rule against the admission of hearsay evidence.

Pursuant to rules such as Rule 703, much (if not all) of an expert's testimony may be based on inadmissible evidence. As long as the evidence is "reasonably reliable," the expert's opinion may be disclosed to the jury. Often that determination is a difficult one for judges to make. It requires judges to evaluate data with which they may be unfamiliar and to deal with fields in which they are not expert. Some courts have been so liberal with this standard that an expert may testify to almost anything as long as it is said to assist the jury.

During cross-examination, you must challenge the validity of the data on which the expert has relied. You can do this by showing documentary evidence that establishes that the expert's opinions are not shared by eminent practitioners in the field.

Your task as the cross-examiner is to discern which facts and assumptions were key to the expert's opinion, and then attack the testimony by showing that the conclusions would be different if the facts were changed or additional facts assumed. A trial court, for example, may exclude testimony if there is no evidence to support the facts underlying the hypothetical question to which the expert responded. And an appellate court can reverse a verdict if the essential facts on which the expert based his or her testimony were contrary to the facts proven in the case.

Attacking the Validity of the Expert's Basis

By exposing the basis underlying the expert's opinion, you can pinpoint the flaws and thereby cast doubt on the expert's opinion.

This technique is especially effective for challenges based on the adequacy of the data employed, errors in calculations, and alternative data not considered.

For example:

> Q: And your opinion is based on the documents you have shown us, is that correct?
>
> A: Yes.
>
> Q: And these documents were given to you by the lawyer for the defendants?
>
> A: Yes.
>
> Q: Don't you think it would be more reasonable to search the literature on your own before you start offering opinions on such complicated matters?

Or like this:

> Q: There were only two doctors who physically examined Ms. Knox's husband after he died—the emergency room physician and the coroner. Is that correct?
>
> A: Yes.
>
> Q: And your opinions were made from an examination of documents produced by other individuals, is that correct?
>
> A: Yes.

Or maybe this:

> Q: But all the evidence points to a leaky valve on the piston. You just didn't find it. There may be fish in the pond. You just didn't catch them because you weren't in the right place. Fair?

Discrediting the Witness

A cross-examiner may first discredit the witness by showing that the witness is not qualified to testify as an expert; i.e., that the expert does not have the requisite knowledge, skill, experience, training, or education. By clarifying the expert's true area of expertise, you can show that the particular area is not directly applicable to the issue on which the expert is testifying. By showing that the witness is not qualified to testify as an expert on the issue at hand, the testimony may be excluded altogether, and at the very least you have reduced the witness' credibility.

Another effective means of discrediting the witness is to show inaccuracies in the expert's opinion or false assumptions and incorrect facts on which the opinion was based. It may be helpful to emphasize a common theme in dramatizing these points. For example, it may be devastating to show that the expert concentrated his or her research only in a specialized area, that the expert has always testified for only one side of the docket, or that the expert is a professional witness and not a practitioner.

Your own expert can be very useful in highlighting the incorrect basis or theories on which the opposing expert's opinion is based, and therefore assist in the preparation of an effective cross-examination. There is no substitute for thorough preparation in the cross-examination of the opposing expert.

Effective Cross-Examination Style

Courts will also exclude expert testimony if it does not assist the trier of fact. Testimony is unhelpful to the jury if it is cumulative, conjectural, speculative, or within the jury's common knowledge. Testimony does not assist the trier of fact if it does not help the jury resolve a controversial issue.

Courts must engage in a Federal Rule of Evidence 403 analysis in such a situation, excluding the evidence if its probative value is substantially outweighed by the danger of unfair prejudice, confusion of the issues, or misleading the jury. The liberality of the federal rules generally resolves all doubts concerning the utility of an expert's testimony in favor of admissibility. The rationale for this approach is that the jury is capable of ignoring unhelpful evidence.

The most effective cross-examination is often confined to focusing on areas omitted on direct examination. Your job is to show that the expert has made prior inconsistent statements or is guilty of bias or prejudice. You can learn enough about the witness's subject matter to take advantage of inconsistencies and distortions, but never be drawn into a battle with the expert on his or her own ground. Your field is the courtroom—hold on to your advantage.

The effectiveness of cross-examination depends largely on your perceptiveness in sensing the mood and reaction of the witness. You must exercise a tight rein on the questioning so that a witness is not free to make lengthy explanations that are beyond your control. Another tactic is to seek an agreement early in the examination requiring the expert to give "yes" or "no" answers. Objecting to an answer as nonresponsive is usually a more appropriate way of avoiding damaging answers than moving to strike.

Subjective Judgment

You should also seek concessions from the expert that the opinion includes some subjective judgment. In any discipline in which judgment is involved, always ask the expert if he or she could be wrong, or if another interpretation is not equally plausible. When seeking concessions, consider using phraseology such as: "As a reasonable person, could you not agree . . . ."

You must be persistent, but respectfully so:

Q: You're a little bit outside your area of expertise as you testify today, aren't you?

A: No, that's not true.

Q: We'll discuss that a little more in a moment, but don't you agree that you were stretching things a bit when you said that the accident was caused by a slippery surface?

A: Not one bit.

Q: Is it possible that maybe you were relying on what the lawyers for Mr. Dowd were telling you instead of what the science teaches?

▼▼▼▼▼

Practice Pointers for Taking Cross-Examination

- ◆ Consider using graduate students in the field to investigate the opposing expert's credentials, publications, and prior testimony. They understand the issues in the field and are less expensive than paralegals.

- ◆ Determine whether the expert advertises, and if so, if such advertising is blatantly shoved toward one side.

- ◆ Ask your nontestifying expert about the opposing expert, and if appropriate, to make inquiries in the field about the opposing expert.

- ◆ Talk to lawyers who have opposed the expert in prior cases.

- ◆ Try to obtain the exhibits used during the expert's testimony in prior cases.

Constructive versus Destructive

Constructive cross-examination should precede destructive cross-examination. It makes more sense to first extract the points that build your argument before challenging the expert's credibility as to the remainder of assertions.

Establish that the expert being cross-examined agrees with your expert in many areas. Specifically present the data and other bases utilized by your expert and ask the opposing expert to agree that they are appropriately and frequently relied on by experts in the field. Establish the limitations imposed on the expert by the demands of litigation. If the expert does not wish to concede a point during constructive cross-examination, reserve it for destructive questioning later.

Keep all questions concise so that the expert can answer with a "yes" or "no" and has no opportunity to explain the answer further. If the question is clear and fair, further explanation by the witness will look like an evasion. If the point is not crucial, you can again ask the witness to restrict the answer to a "yes" or "no."

To establish the proper tone, begin with a topic of moderate importance on which you have absolutely controlling material, such as deposition testimony. To make a point so that the judge and jury appreciate what you are teaching them, emphasize facts that the expert has not utilized in his or her analysis. Impeach crisply and then move on. Use a series of shorter questions instead of a long conclusory question.

Do not let the opposing expert leave the witness chair to provide drawings or other demonstrative aids. You do not want the expert to have the opportunity to be interesting or persuasive.

Attacking the Expert's Credentials

Start by showing where the expert is *not* qualified:

> Q: Let me make sure I have this clear. Number one, you are not a medical scientist, correct?
> A: Yes, that's true.
> Q: Number two, you are not qualified to compute what these studies say?
> A: That's correct.
> Q: So you rely on Dr. Sawrell to tell you what the scientific studies reveal?
> A: Yes.

Information Admitted into Evidence

An expert can base an opinion on facts to which other witnesses have testified at trial. This category includes documents, exhibits, facts, data, and opinions admitted through other witnesses. The expert may thus base an opinion on certain assumptions or facts advanced at trial, elicited by a hypothetical question, or heard by the expert in attendance at the trial.

You should pinpoint exactly which facts the expert has relied on and which facts the expert has omitted in arriving at the opinion expressed. You may also rebut the expert's opinion by revealing incorrect or inadequate factual assumptions, or by showing that the expert used incorrect or inadequate reasoning in reaching the stated conclusions.

As cross-examiner you should modify the facts given to the expert to determine if her opinion changes. You could ask, for example, "What if assumption X was not true?" You also may ask your own hypothetical, which, if properly formulated, is likely to elicit a response favorable to your position.

For example:

Q: Don't you think it would be a little more reasonable, before you start offering opinions to the jury, to do your own research rather than rely on that of the lawyers?

Information Not Admitted into Evidence

Experts often base their opinions on information presented to them outside the courtroom or even outside their own perception. Under the evidentiary rules of most jurisdictions, this otherwise inadmissible evidence is admitted if the information is of a type reasonably relied on by experts in the field. This category encompasses the kind of information that experts rely on professionally when forming opinions.

On the other hand, an expert may not base his or her opinion on statistics that were prepared for litigation but did not form part of an independent study; on affidavits based on unsupported assumptions; or on testimony of parties and witnesses at the scene of the accident.

Even if the court finds that experts in the field reasonably rely on the evidence used by the expert, you may still attempt to establish that the opinion is nonetheless unreliable. Thus, although it may be reasonable for a physician to rely on statements made to him by his patient, as cross-examiner you may choose to portray the statement itself as unreliable.

Statistics

You may find it necessary to carefully examine an expert's reliance on statistics, data, studies, polls, and calculations, and show they are unreliable and lack probative value. In addition, even if experts in the particular field regularly rely on a particular type of data, the methodology used to develop the data may be unreliable. You may show, for example, that the data do not include all essential factors, or that the expert compiled the data solely for litigation purposes.

The cross-examiner below effectively accomplishes this:

Q: You examined the slides made from Mr. Johnson's heart?
A: Yes.
Q: How many slides are there?
A: Several dozen.
Q: That's all you looked at?
A: Yes.
Q: And you haven't looked at all the blood vessels in this left ventricular area to see if there is a clot, have you?
A: I looked at enough to be a statistical sample that would be sufficient to make my conclusions.
Q: How many?
A: Maybe 1,000.
Q: How many are there in all?
A: Maybe 150,000.
Q: And you only looked at 1,000?
A: Yes.
Q: So there were tens of thousands of cuts you did not look at, right?
A: Right.

Learned Treatises

Most jurisdictions provide a hearsay exception for the substantive admissibility of statements contained in learned treatises: If a work is established as a reliable authority by the testimony of the expert you are cross-examining, then relevant portions may be read into the record as substantive evidence. Federal Rule of Evidence 803(18) imposes three conditions on admissibility: (1) the expert must establish that the treatise constitutes a reliable authority; (2) the treatise must be called to the attention of an expert witness on cross-examination; and (3) the relevant statements, when admitted, may be read in evidence but may not be received as exhibits.

When a witness relies on an authoritative treatise to form the basis of his or her opinion, you may inquire as to the sources that were available to the witness, those used to form the opinion, and those neglected. If the expert recognizes the treatises as authoritative, you may use them to contradict or impeach the witness, regardless of whether the witness relied on them.

Exposing Personal Bias or Interest

A common way to discredit the expert is to establish a bias in favor of, or a personal interest in, the party for whom the expert is testifying. Although you know that the expert is a hired gun, the jury may not. You should therefore inquire into the fees charged, whether the fees have been paid, and the frequency with which the expert testifies for this particular party or lawyer.

You can show this bias without being overly contentious:

> Q: And you are on the board of a company called Actelion, aren't you?
> A: Absolutely.
> Q: And that's a company with an exclusive worldwide alliance and partnership for research?
> A: They have a number of research associates.
> Q: But they have one that is exclusive. Why don't you tell the jury who their exclusive relationship is with.
> A: They have a relationship with Aacme.
> Q: Aacme.
> A: But I don't believe my work with Actelion has anything to do with what we're talking about today.

Q: Just in the interest of fair play, it doesn't hurt the jury to know about it. You are on the board of a company that is so proud of the relationship they have with Aacme that they have put it in their annual report, where they list your name, by the way.

Exposing Materials Reviewed by the Expert

A deft cross-examiner can reveal the paucity of material examined by the expert:

Q: If we were to take a ballpark look at what materials were given to you by the Aacme lawyers for your review versus what you found on your own, we would have these two stacks, wouldn't we?

Preparing Your Expert for Cross-Examination

The shoe is now on the other foot and you must defend your expert on cross-examination by opposing counsel. Above all, your expert must be able to maintain credibility as an independent witness who does not have a stake in the outcome of the case. Your job is to help your expert weather grueling cross-examination without losing her temper, changing her conclusions, or becoming defensive and overstating her views.

The following checklist is designed to help your expert understand some ground rules and pointers to enhance the persuasive impact of your testimony.

You should tell experts:

♦ That if asked whether they talked with an lawyer about the case, the answer is that of course they spoke with an lawyer.

♦ Not to offer any opinions that they are not qualified to express and to freely acknowledge the limits of their expertise.

- Not to guess, not to exaggerate their opinion, and not to be afraid to admit that they don't know the answer.
- To prepare their answers before speaking, to double-check their answers against any records they may have with them, and to pause briefly before answering the question to give you an opportunity to object.
- Not to allow themselves to be forced into a flat "yes" or "no" answer if a qualified answer is necessary to make it truthful.
- To be prepared to explain each step of their analysis and how long each step took.
- To be prepared to explain why certain tests were not performed.
- To be prepared to explain why they disagree with other authorities in the field.
- To avoid referring to any source as authoritative, but instead acknowledge it as helpful in some areas.
- To be prepared to discuss fees without equivocation.

Confusing Questions

Your witness can expect that various trick or confusing questions may be asked. These include:

Compound questions: If one question is buried in another, the witness should ask the opposing lawyer to separate them before he or she answers.

Double negatives: The potential for confusion is obvious.

Misquotations or mischaracterizations: This is especially damaging if it purports to be the expert's own prior testimony or publications. The expert should correct even minor deviations.

Intervening or independently sufficient causes: A common trick question involves introducing intervening or independently sufficient causes within a hypothetical question. If some of the conditions posed deviate significantly from the facts, the expert should bring this to counsel's attention.

Insufficient hypothetical questions: Hypothetical questions posed on cross-examination often do not contain enough information or the right information to support a conclusion. The expert should state what is missing or that that the question cannot be answered as asked.

General, broad questions: The witness should answer accurately, truthfully, and as briefly as possible.

▼▼▼▼▼

Practice Pointers for Defending Cross-Examination

There are several things for an expert to consider as questions are being answered. Experts should be reminded that they

- Need not answer every question, and that it is fine to admit that they do not know the answer.

- Should listen carefully to the entire question, and not answer until they are sure they understand the question.

- Should not answer if you have objected to it until the judge has ruled on it.

- Should not volunteer information not specifically asked for, without being too abrupt or hostile.

- Should qualify their answer if that is necessary for them to give an accurate and truthful answer.

- Should give factual information in answer to a question only if they have knowledge of the facts.

- Should answer all questions truthfully.

- Should not exaggerate.

- Should be objective and impartial.

- Should not try to bluff.

- Should not be smug.

- Should be reasonable and fair.

Courtroom Simulation

To relieve the expert's nervousness about cross-examination, you should conduct a simulated cross-examination of the witness. The simulated examination should conform, both in form and substance, to the rules of procedure and evidence that will apply at trial. To the extent possible, you should mimic the style of opposing counsel.

The questions should be asked as closely as possible to the anticipated wording of opposing counsel. This may help to avoid the common problem of misunderstanding the question. You and the expert should discuss ways in which the expert can effectively counter questions with the least damage to the direct testimony.

Any practice cross-examination should include the common "trick" questions, such as whether the witness was paid to testify and whether the expert conferred with counsel before testifying. You should attempt to confuse and frustrate the witness just as the opposing counsel is likely to do at trial.

You should also highlight those areas in which the expert and the opponent's expert are in agreement. The expert should be warned not to expect a trick in every question and that it is acceptable to agree with opposing counsel in proper circumstances. The expert should control his or her temper. If a cross-examining lawyer can provoke a display of anger or sarcasm, he or she will have succeeded in discrediting the expert's testimony. The expert should not show exasperation, boredom, fatigue, or surprise.

The object is for the expert to project an air of professionalism and reasonable confidence that will persuade the jury that she knows what she is talking about.

Retaining Control

The expert should never let the cross-examiner put words in his mouth, as shown by this experienced expert:

> Q: There's a good reason why the condition doesn't happen often in your sleep, isn't there?

A: I don't agree with your characterization that it doesn't happen often in your sleep.

The expert should not let her main point get lost:

A: The fact is that Mr. Davis had been smoking for thirty years. And at the end of the day, the risk score wasn't very accurate because Mr. Davis had moderate to severe arteriosclerosis. That is the fact in this case, regardless of what we say the average risk score is.

Pointing out the slanted language of the cross-examiner is an effective technique:

Q: Where do you get the idea that there's no evidence in the world that the drug causes sudden cardiac death?
A: I hope the jury heard that phrase, "there's no evidence in the world."

I didn't say there was no evidence in the world. But I think that if you look at the totality of the evidence, there is no convincing study that shows that the drug increases the chances of sudden cardiac death.

The expert may have to show the complexity of the issue:

Q: I don't think what you've stated accurately reflects the study.
A: I think that this is the kind of study in which the results are very difficult to interpret.

In fact, the expert may have to be quite blunt in response:

A: You are mischaracterizing my testimony. The jury has to listen very carefully here. I am talking about sudden cardiac death, and you are talking about all cardiac events.

Concluding questions give the expert an excellent opening to respond:

Q: Wouldn't you agree with me that Mr. Charles died because he wasn't getting enough oxygenated blood to his heart?

A: No. I'd have to use my own words. I wouldn't even come close to using those words. I think Mr. Charles had advanced arteriosclerosis. I think there was evidence that he had chronic ischemia. And the autopsy showed that he had fibrosis.

Responding to Questions About Bias

The cross-examiner will inevitably try to show bias. Here is a nice riposte:

Q: You work for Pharma, do you not?
A: Yes.
Q: And you also do work for the FDA?
A: That's correct.
Q: Your FDA work would be very valuable to Pharma, would it not?
A: Yes, my knowledge is useful for developing new drugs.
Q: And Pharma has a friend on the FDA giving approval to new drugs, don't they?
A: If you are implying that my service to the FDA gives unfair advantage to Pharma, you are mistaken. There is scrutiny from FDA lawyers on everything we are involved with. And the record speaks for itself. The FDA turns down more drugs from Pharma than it accepts.

Responding to Questions About Treatises

It is important *never* to admit the authority of a treatise, despite the pressure of the cross-examination:

Q: Rubin on pathology is one of the bibles of your field, isn't it?
A: It's a pathology textbook, and is widely recognized.
Q: It is clearly an authority, isn't it?
A: No.
Q: You don't consider it an authority.
A: No. All textbooks are a summation of reading the literature and making analysis. They are opinions of the author. Certain things are correct, and other things are incorrect.

Responding to Questions About Fees

Admitting without guilt that one is paid is effective.

> Q: You have been paid by the company for consulting, haven't you?
> A: Absolutely.

Responding to Questions About Income

Here is a good way to handle the income question:

> A: My total income is stated clearly on those tax returns. It's not pleasant to discuss your own income in public, since most people consider it a matter of some privacy. I have been a very fortunate individual with my work, and that is my income, which I work hard to earn.

Appendix A:
William Daubert v.
Merrell Dow
Pharmaceuticals, Inc.
509 U.S. 579 (1993)

Justice BLACKMUN delivered the opinion of the Court.

In this case, we are called upon to determine the standard for admitting expert scientific testimony in a federal trial.

I.

Petitioners Jason Daubert and Eric Schuller are minor children born with serious birth defects. They and their parents sued respondent in California state court, alleging that the birth defects had been caused by the mothers' ingestion of Bendectin, a prescription anti nausea drug marketed by respondent. Respondent removed the suits to federal court on diversity grounds.

After extensive discovery, respondent moved for summary judgment, contending that Bendectin does not cause birth defects in humans and that petitioners would be unable to come forward with any admissible evidence that it does. In support of its motion, respondent submitted an affidavit of Steven H. Lamm, physician and epidemiologist, who is a well credentialed expert on the risks from exposure to various chemical substances.[1] Doctor Lamm stated that he had reviewed all the literature on Bendectin and human birth defects—more than 30 published studies involving over 130,000 patients. No study had found Bendectin to be a human teratogen (*i.e.,* a substance capable of causing malformations in fetuses). On the basis of this review, Doctor Lamm concluded that maternal use of Bendectin during the first trimester of pregnancy has not been shown to be a risk factor for human birth defects.

Petitioners did not (and do not) contest this characterization of the published record regarding Bendectin. Instead, they responded to respondent's motion with the testimony of eight experts of their own, each of whom also possessed impressive credentials.[2] These experts had concluded that Bendectin can cause birth defects. Their conclusions were based upon "in vitro" (test tube) and "in vivo" (live) animal studies that found a link between Bendectin and malformations; pharmacological studies of the chemical structure of Bendectin that purported to show similarities between the structure of the drug and that of other substances known to cause birth defects; and the "reanalysis" of previously published epidemiological (human statistical) studies.

The District Court granted respondent's motion for summary judgment. The court stated that scientific evidence is admissible only if the principle upon which it is based is " 'sufficiently established to have general acceptance in the field to which it belongs.' " 727 F. Supp. 570, 572 (SD Cal. 1989), quoting *United States* v. *Kilgus,* 571 F.2d 508, 510 (CA9 1978). The court concluded that petitioners' evidence did not meet this standard. Given the vast body of epidemiological data concerning Bendectin, the court held, expert opinion which is not based on epidemiological evidence is not admissible to establish causation. 727 F. Supp., at 575. Thus, the animal cell studies, live animal studies, and chemical structure analyses on which petitioners had relied could not raise by themselves a reasonably disputable jury issue regarding causation. *Ibid.* Petitioners' epidemiological analyses, based as they were on recalculations of data in previously published studies that had found no causal link between the drug and birth defects, were ruled to be inadmissible because they had not been published or subjected to peer review. *Ibid.*

The United States Court of Appeals for the Ninth Circuit affirmed. 951 F.2d 1128 (1991). Citing *Frye* v. *United States,* 54 App. D.C. 46, 47, 293 F. 1013, 1014 (1923), the court stated that expert opinion based on a scientific technique is inadmissible unless the technique is "generally accepted" as reliable in the relevant scientific community. 951 F.2d, at 1129–1130. The court declared that expert opinion based on a methodology that diverges "significantly from the procedures accepted by recognized authorities in the field . . . cannot be shown to be `generally accepted as a reliable technique.'" *Id.,* at 1130, quoting *United States* v. *Solomon,* 753 F.2d 1522, 1526 (CA9 1985).

The court emphasized that other Courts of Appeals considering the risks of Bendectin had refused to admit reanalyses of epidemiological studies that had been neither published nor subjected to peer review. 951 F.2d, at 1130–1131. Those courts had found unpublished reanalyses "particularly problematic in light of the massive weight of the original published studies supporting [respondent's] position, all of which had undergone full scrutiny from the scientific community." *Id.,* at 1130. Contending that reanalysis is generally accepted by the scientific community only when it is subjected to verification and scrutiny by others in the field, the Court of Appeals rejected petitioners' reanalyses as "unpublished, not subjected to the normal peer review process and generated solely for use in litigation." *Id.,* at 1131. The court concluded that petitioners' evidence provided an insufficient foundation to allow admission of expert testimony that Bendectin caused their injuries and, accordingly, that petitioners could not satisfy their burden of proving causation at trial.

We granted certiorari, 506 U.S. 914, 113 S. Ct. 320, 121 L. Ed. 2d 240 (1992), in light of sharp divisions among the courts regarding the proper standard for the admission of expert testimony.

Compare, *e. g., United States* v. *Shorter,* 257 U. S. App. D.C. 358, 363–364, 809 F.2d 54, 59–60 (applying the "general acceptance" standard), cert. denied, 484 U.S. 817 (1987), with *DeLuca* v. *Merrell Dow Pharmaceuticals, Inc.,* 911 F.2d 941, 955 (CA3 1990) (rejecting the "general acceptance" standard).

II.
A.

In the 70 years since its formulation in the *Frye* case, the "general acceptance" test has been the dominant standard for determining the admissibility of novel scientific evidence at trial. See E. Green & C. Nesson, Problems, Cases, and Materials on Evidence 649 (1983). Although under increasing attack of late, the rule continues to be followed by a majority of courts, including the Ninth Circuit.[3]

The *Frye* test has its origin in a short and citation free 1923 decision concerning the admissibility of evidence derived from a systolic blood pressure deception test, a crude precursor to the polygraph machine. In what has become a famous (perhaps infamous) passage, the then Court of Appeals for the District of Columbia described the device and its operation and declared:

> "Just when a scientific principle or discovery crosses the line between the experimental and demonstrable stages is difficult to define. Somewhere in this twilight zone the evidential force of the principle must be recognized, and while courts will go a long way in admitting expert testimony deduced from a well recognized scientific principle or discovery, *the thing from which the deduction is made must be sufficiently established to have gained general acceptance in the particular field in which it belongs.*" 54 App. D.C., at 47, 293 F., at 1014 (emphasis added).

Because the deception test had "not yet gained such standing and scientific recognition among physiological and psychological authorities as would justify the courts in admitting expert testimony deduced from the discovery, development, and experiments thus far made," evidence of its results was ruled inadmissible. *Ibid.*

The merits of the *Frye* test have been much debated, and scholarship on its proper scope and application is legion.[4] Petitioners' primary attack, however, is not on the content but on the continuing authority of the rule. They contend that the *Frye* test was superseded by the adoption of the Federal Rules of Evidence.[5] We agree.

We interpret the legislatively enacted Federal Rules of Evidence as we would any statute. *Beech Aircraft Corp.* v. *Rainey,* 488 U.S. 153, 163 (1988). Rule 402 provides the baseline:

> "All relevant evidence is admissible, except as otherwise provided by the Constitution of the United States, by Act of Congress, by these rules, or by other rules prescribed by the Supreme Court pursuant to statutory authority. Evidence which is not relevant is not admissible."

"Relevant evidence" is defined as that which has "any tendency to make the existence of any fact that is of consequence to the determination of the action more probable or less probable than it would be without the evidence." Rule 401. The Rule's basic standard of relevance thus is a liberal one.

Frye, of course, predated the Rules by half a century. In *United States* v. *Abel,* 469 U.S. 45 (1984), we considered the pertinence of background common law in interpreting the Rules of Evidence. We noted that the Rules occupy the field, *id.,* at 49, but, quoting Professor Cleary, the Reporter, explained that the common law nevertheless could serve as an aid to their application:

> " 'In principle, under the Federal Rules no common law of evidence remains. 'All relevant evidence is admissible, except as otherwise provided . . . .' In reality, of course, the body of common law knowledge continues to exist, though in the somewhat altered form of a source of guidance in the exercise of delegated powers.' " *Id.,* at 51–52.

We found the common law precept at issue in the *Abel* case entirely consistent with Rule 402's general requirement of admissibility, and considered it unlikely that the drafters had intended to change the rule. *Id.,* at 50–51. In *Bourjaily* v. *United States,* 483

U.S. 171 (1987), on the other hand, the Court was unable to find a particular common law doctrine in the Rules, and so held it superseded.

Here there is a specific Rule that speaks to the contested issue. Rule 702, governing expert testimony, provides:

> "If scientific, technical, or other specialized knowledge will assist the trier of fact to understand the evidence or to determine a fact in issue, a witness qualified as an expert by knowledge, skill, experience, training, or education, may testify thereto in the form of an opinion or otherwise."

Nothing in the text of this Rule establishes "general acceptance" as an absolute prerequisite to admissibility. Nor does respondent present any clear indication that Rule 702 or the Rules as a whole were intended to incorporate a "general acceptance" standard. The drafting history makes no mention of *Frye,* and a rigid "general acceptance" requirement would be at odds with the "liberal thrust" of the Federal Rules and their "general approach of relaxing the traditional barriers to 'opinion' testimony." *Beech Aircraft Corp.* v. *Rainey,* 488 U.S., at 169 (citing Rules 701 to 705). See also Weinstein, Rule 702 of the Federal Rules of Evidence is Sound; It Should Not Be Amended, 138 F.R.D. 631, 631 (1991) ("The Rules were designed to depend primarily upon lawyer adversaries and sensible triers of fact to evaluate conflicts"). Given the Rules' permissive backdrop and their inclusion of a specific rule on expert testimony that does not mention "general acceptance," the assertion that the Rules somehow assimilated *Frye* is unconvincing. *Frye* made 'general acceptance' the exclusive test for admitting expert scientific testimony. That austere standard, absent from and incompatible with the Federal Rules of Evidence, should not be applied in federal trials.[6]

B.

That the *Frye* test was displaced by the Rules of Evidence does not mean, however, that the Rules themselves place no limits on the admissibility of purportedly scientific evidence.[7] Nor is the trial judge disabled from screening such evidence. To the contrary, under the Rules the trial judge must ensure that any and all scientific testimony or evidence admitted is not only relevant, but reliable.

The primary locus of this obligation is Rule 702, which clearly contemplates some degree of regulation of the subjects and theories about which an expert may testify. "*If scientific,* technical, or other specialized *knowledge will assist the trier of fact* to understand the evidence or to determine a fact in issue" an expert "may testify *thereto.*" The subject of an expert's testimony must be "scientific . . . knowledge."[8] The adjective "scientific" implies a grounding in the methods and procedures of science. Similarly, the word "knowledge" connotes more than subjective belief or unsupported speculation. The term "applies to any body of known facts or to any body of ideas inferred from such facts or accepted as truths on good grounds." Webster's Third New International Dictionary 1252 (1986). Of course, it would be unreasonable to conclude that the subject of scientific testimony must be "known" to a certainty; arguably, there are no certainties in science. See, *e. g.,* Brief for Nicolaas Bloembergen et al. as *Amici Curiae* 9 ("Indeed, scientists do not assert that they know what is immutably 'true'—they are committed to searching for new, temporary theories to explain, as best they can, phenomena"); Brief for American Association for the Advancement of Science and the National Academy of Sciences as *Amici Curiae* 7–8 ("Science is not an encyclopedic body of knowledge about the universe. Instead, it represents a *process* for proposing and refining theoretical explanations about the world that are subject to further testing and refinement") (emphasis in original). But, in order to qualify as "scientific knowledge," an inference or assertion must be derived by the scientific method. Proposed testimony must be supported by appropriate validation—*i.e.,* "good grounds," based on what is known. In short, the requirement that an expert's testimony pertain to "scientific knowledge" establishes a standard of evidentiary reliability.[9]

Rule 702 further requires that the evidence or testimony "assist the trier of fact to understand the evidence or to determine a fact in issue." This condition goes primarily to relevance. "Expert testimony which does not relate to any issue in the case is not relevant and, ergo, non helpful." 3 Weinstein & Berger ¶ 702[02], p. 702–18. See also *United States* v. *Downing,* 753 F.2d 1224, 1242 (CA3 1985) ("An additional consideration under Rule 702—and another aspect of relevancy—is whether expert testimony proffered in the case is sufficiently tied to the facts of the case that it will aid the jury in resolving a factual dispute"). The consideration has been aptly described by Judge Becker as one of "fit." *Ibid.* "Fit" is not always obvious, and scientific validity for one purpose is not necessarily scientific validity for other, unrelated purposes. See Starrs, *Frye* v. *United States* Restructured and Revitalized: A Proposal to Amend Federal Evidence Rule 702, and 26 Jurimetrics J. 249, 258 (1986). The study of the phases of the moon, for example, may provide valid scientific "knowledge" about whether a certain night was dark, and if darkness is a fact in issue, the knowledge will assist the trier of fact. However (absent creditable grounds supporting such a link), evidence that the moon was full on a certain night will not assist the trier of fact in determining whether an individual was unusually likely to have behaved irrationally on that night. Rule 702's "helpfulness" standard requires a valid scientific connection to the pertinent inquiry as a precondition to admissibility.

That these requirements are embodied in Rule 702 is not surprising. Unlike an ordinary witness, see Rule 701, an expert is permitted wide latitude to offer opinions, including those that are not based on first hand knowledge or observation. See Rules 702 and 703. Presumably, this relaxation of the usual requirement of first hand knowledge—a rule which represents "a 'most pervasive manifestation' of the common law insistence upon 'the most reliable sources of information,'" Advisory Committee's Notes on Fed. Rule Evid. 602 (citation omitted)—is premised on an assumption that the expert's opinion will have a reliable basis in the knowledge and experience of his discipline.

C.

Faced with a proffer of expert scientific testimony, then, the trial judge must determine at the outset, pursuant to Rule 104(a),[10] whether the expert is proposing to testify to (1) scientific knowledge that (2) will assist the trier of fact to understand or determine a fact in issue.[11] This entails a preliminary assessment of whether the reasoning or methodology underlying the testimony is scientifically valid and of whether that reasoning or methodology properly can be applied to the facts in issue. We are confident that federal judges possess the capacity to undertake this review. Many factors will bear on the inquiry, and we do not presume to set out a definitive checklist or test. But some general observations are appropriate.

Ordinarily, a key question to be answered in determining whether a theory or technique is scientific knowledge that will assist the trier of fact will be whether it can be (and has been) tested. "Scientific methodology today is based on generating hypotheses and testing them to see if they can be falsified; indeed, this methodology is what distinguishes science from other fields of human inquiry." Green, at 645. See also C. Hempel, Philosophy of Natural Science 49 (1966) ("[T]he statements constituting a scientific explanation must be capable of empirical test"); K. Popper, Conjectures and Refutations: The Growth of Scientific Knowledge 37 (5th ed. 1989) ("[T]he criterion of the scientific status of a theory is its falsifiability, or refutability, or testability").

Another pertinent consideration is whether the theory or technique has been subjected to peer review and publication. Publication (which is but one element of peer review) is not a *sine qua non* of admissibility; it does not necessarily correlate with reliability, see S. Jasanoff, The Fifth Branch: Science Advisors as Policymakers 61–76 (1990), and in some instances well grounded but innovative theories will not have been published, see Horrobin, The Philosophical Basis of Peer Review and the Suppression of Innovation, 263 JAMA 1438 (1990). Some propositions, moreover, are too particular, too new, or of too limited interest to be published. But submission to the scrutiny of the scientific community is a component of "good science," in part because it increases the likelihood that substantive flaws in methodology will be detected. See J. Ziman, Reliable Knowledge: An Exploration of the Grounds for Belief in Science 130–133 (1978); Relman and Angell, How Good Is Peer Review?, 321 New Eng. J. Med. 827 (1989). The fact of publication (or lack thereof) in a peer reviewed journal thus will be a relevant, though not dispositive, consideration in assessing the scientific validity of a particular technique or methodology on which an opinion is premised.

Additionally, in the case of a particular scientific technique, the court ordinarily should consider the known or potential rate of error, see, *e. g., United States* v. *Smith,* 869 F.2d 348, 353–354 (CA7 1989) (surveying studies of the error rate of spectrographic voice identification technique), and the existence and maintenance of standards controlling the technique's operation. See *United States* v. *Williams,* 583 F.2d 1194, 1198 (CA2 1978) (noting professional organization's standard governing spectrographic analysis), cert. denied, 439 U.S. 1117 (1979).

Finally, "general acceptance" can yet have a bearing on the inquiry. A "reliability assessment does not require, although it does permit, explicit identification of a relevant scientific community and an express determination of a particular degree of acceptance within that community." *United States* v. *Downing,* 753 F.2d, at 1238. See also 3 Weinstein & Berger ¶ 702[03], pp. 702–41 to 702–42. Widespread acceptance can be an important factor in ruling particular evidence admissible, and "a known technique that has been able to attract only minimal support within the community," *Downing, supra,* at 1238, may properly be viewed with skepticism.

The inquiry envisioned by Rule 702 is, we emphasize, a flexible one.[12] Its overarching subject is the scientific validity—and thus the evidentiary relevance and reliability—of the principles that underlie a proposed submission. The focus, of course, must be solely on principles and methodology, not on the conclusions that they generate.

Throughout, a judge assessing a proffer of expert scientific testimony under Rule 702 should also be mindful of other applicable rules. Rule 703 provides that expert opinions based on otherwise inadmissible hearsay are to be admitted only if the facts or data are "of a type reasonably relied upon by experts in the particular field in forming opinions or inferences upon the subject." Rule 706 allows the court at its discretion to procure the assistance of an expert of its own choosing. Finally, Rule 403 permits the exclusion of relevant evidence "if its probative value is substantially outweighed by the danger of unfair prejudice,

confusion of the issues, or misleading the jury . . . ." Judge Weinstein has explained: "Expert evidence can be both powerful and
quite misleading because of the difficulty in evaluating it.
Because of this risk, the judge in weighing possible prejudice
against probative force under Rule 403 of the present rules exer-
cises more control over experts than over lay witnesses." Weinstein, 138 F.R.D., at 632.

III.

We conclude by briefly addressing what appear to be two underlying concerns of the parties and *amici* in this case. Respondent
expresses apprehension that abandonment of "general acceptance" as the exclusive requirement for admission will result in a
"free for all" in which befuddled juries are confounded by absurd
and irrational pseudoscientific assertions. In this regard respondent seems to us to be overly pessimistic about the capabilities
of the jury, and of the adversary system generally. Vigorous cross
examination, presentation of contrary evidence, and careful
instruction on the burden of proof are the traditional and appropriate means of attacking shaky but admissible evidence. See
Rock v. *Arkansas,* 483 U.S. 44, 61 (1987). Additionally, in the event
the trial court concludes that the scintilla of evidence presented
supporting a position is insufficient to allow a reasonable juror to
conclude that the position more likely than not is true, the court
remains free to direct a judgment, Fed. Rule Civ. Proc. 50 (a), and
likewise to grant summary judgment, Fed. Rule Civ. Proc. 56. Cf.,
e.g., Turpin v. *Merrell Dow Pharmaceuticals, Inc.,* 959 F.2d 1349
(CA6) (holding that scientific evidence that provided foundation
for expert testimony, viewed in the light most favorable to plaintiffs, was not sufficient to allow a jury to find it more probable
than not that defendant caused plaintiff's injury), cert. denied,
506 U.S. 826, 113 S. Ct. 84, 121 L. Ed. 2d 47 (1992); *Brock* v. *Merrell
Dow Pharmaceuticals, Inc.,* 874 F.2d 307 (CA5 1989) (reversing
judgment entered on jury verdict for plaintiffs because evidence
regarding causation was insufficient), modified, 884 F.2d 166 (CA5
1989), cert. denied, 494 U.S. 1046 (1990); Green 680–681. These
conventional devices, rather than wholesale exclusion under an
uncompromising "general acceptance" test, are the appropriate

safeguards where the basis of scientific testimony meets the standards of Rule 702.

Petitioners and, to a greater extent, their *amici* exhibit a different concern. They suggest that recognition of a screening role for the judge that allows for the exclusion of "invalid" evidence will sanction a stifling and repressive scientific orthodoxy and will be inimical to the search for truth. See, *e.g.,* Brief for Ronald Bayer et al. as *Amici Curiae.* It is true that open debate is an essential part of both legal and scientific analyses. Yet there are important differences between the quest for truth in the courtroom and the quest for truth in the laboratory. Scientific conclusions are subject to perpetual revision. Law, on the other hand, must resolve disputes finally and quickly. The scientific project is advanced by broad and wide ranging consideration of a multitude of hypotheses, for those that are incorrect will eventually be shown to be so, and that in itself is an advance. Conjectures that are probably wrong are of little use, however, in the project of reaching a quick, final, and binding legal judgment—often of great consequence—about a particular set of events in the past. We recognize that in practice, a gatekeeping role for the judge, no matter how flexible, inevitably on occasion will prevent the jury from learning of authentic insights and innovations. That, nevertheless, is the balance that is struck by Rules of Evidence designed not for the exhaustive search for cosmic understanding but for the particularized resolution of legal disputes.[13]

IV.

To summarize: "general acceptance" is not a necessary precondition to the admissibility of scientific evidence under the Federal Rules of Evidence, but the Rules of Evidence—especially Rule 702—do assign to the trial judge the task of ensuring that an expert's testimony both rests on a reliable foundation and is relevant to the task at hand. Pertinent evidence based on scientifically valid principles will satisfy those demands.

The inquiries of the District Court and the Court of Appeals focused almost exclusively on "general acceptance," as gauged by publication and the decisions of other courts. Accordingly, the judgment of the Court of Appeals is vacated and the case is remanded for further proceedings consistent with this opinion. It is so ordered.

Notes

1. Doctor Lamm received his master's and doctor of medicine degrees from the University of Southern California. He has served as a consultant in birth defect epidemiology for the National Center for Health Statistics and has published numerous articles on the magnitude of risk from exposure to various chemical and biological substances. App. 34–44.

2. For example, Shanna Helen Swan, who received a master's degree in biostatics from Columbia University and a doctorate in statistics from the University of California at Berkeley, is chief of the section of the California Department of Health and Services that determines causes of birth defects, and has served as a consultant to the World Health Organization, the Food and Drug Administration, and the National Institutes of Health. App. 113–114, 131–132. Stuart A. Newman, who received his bachelor's in chemistry from Columbia University and his master's and doctorate in chemistry from the University of Chicago, is a professor at New York Medical College and has spent over a decade studying the effect of chemicals on limb development. App. 54–56. The credentials of the others are similarly impressive. See App. 61–66, 73–80, 148–153, 187–192, and Attachment to Petitioners' Opposition to Summary Judgment, Tabs 12, 20, 21, 26, 31, 32.

3. For a catalogue of the many cases on either side of this controversy, see P. Giannelli & E. Imwinkelried, Scientific Evidence § 1-5, pp. 10–14 (1986 & Supp. 1991).

4. See, *e. g.,* Green, Expert Witnesses and Sufficiency of Evidence in Toxic Substances Litigation: The Legacy of *Agent Orange* and Bendectin Litigation, 86 Nw. U. L. Rev. 643 (1992) (hereinafter Green); Becker & Orenstein, The Federal Rules of Evidence After Sixteen Years—The Effect of "Plain Meaning" Jurisprudence, the Need for an Advisory Committee on the Rules of Evidence, and Suggestions for Selective Revision of the Rules, 60 Geo. Wash. L. Rev. 857, 876–885 (1992); Hanson, "James Alphonzo Frye is Sixty-Five Years Old; Should He Retire?," 16 W. St. U. L. Rev. 357 (1989); Black, A Unified Theory of Scientific Evidence, 56 Ford.

L. Rev. 595 (1988); Imwinkelried, The "Bases" of Expert Testimony: The Syllogistic Structure of Scientific Testimony, 67 N.C. L. Rev. 1 (1988); Proposals for a Model Rule on the Admissibility of Scientific Evidence, 26 Jurimetrics J. 235 (1986); Giannelli, The Admissibility of Novel Scientific Evidence: *Frye* v. *United States,* A Half Century Later, 80 Colum. L. Rev. 1197 (1980); The Supreme Court, 1986 Term, 101 Harv. L. Rev. 7, 119, 125–127 (1987).

Indeed, the debates over *Frye* are such a well established part of the academic landscape that a distinct term——"*Frye*ologist"—has been advanced to describe those who take part. See Behringer, Introduction, Proposals for a Model Rule on the Admissibility of Scientific Evidence, 26 Jurimetrics J., at 239, quoting Lacey, Scientific Evidence, 24 Jurimetrics J. 254, 264 (1984).

5. Like the question of *Frye*'s merit, the dispute over its survival has divided courts and commentators. Compare, *e. g., United States* v. *Williams,* 583 F.2d 1194 (CA2 1978), cert. denied, 439 U.S. 1117 (1979) (*Frye* is superseded by the Rules of Evidence), with *Christophersen* v. *Allied Signal Corp.,* 939 F.2d 1106, 1111, 1115–1116 (CA5 1991) (en banc) (*Frye* and the Rules coexist), cert. denied, 503 U.S. 912 (1992), 3 J. Weinstein & M. Berger, Weinstein's Evidence ¶ 702[03], pp. 702–36 to 702–37 (1988) (hereinafter Weinstein & Berger) (*Frye* is dead), and M. Graham, Handbook of Federal Evidence § 703.2 (2d ed. 1991) (*Frye* lives). See generally P. Giannelli & E. Imwinkelried, Scientific Evidence § 1-5, pp. 28–29 (1986 & Supp. 1991) (citing authorities).

6. Because we hold that *Frye* has been superseded and base the discussion that follows on the content of the congressionally enacted Federal Rules of Evidence, we do not address petitioners' argument that application of the *Frye* rule in this diversity case, as the application of a judge made rule affecting substantive rights, would violate the doctrine of *Erie R. Co.* v. *Tompkins,* 304 U.S. 64 (1938).

7. The Chief Justice "do[es] not doubt that Rule 702 confides to the judge some gatekeeping responsibility," *post,* at 4, but would neither say how it does so, nor explain what that role entails. We believe the better course is to note the nature and source of the duty.

8. Rule 702 also applies to "technical, or other specialized knowledge." Our discussion is limited to the scientific context because that is the nature of the expertise offered here.

9. We note that scientists typically distinguish between "validity" (does the principle support what it purports to show?) and "reliability" (does application of the principle produce consistent results?). See Black, A Unified Theory of Scientific Evidence, 56 Ford. L. Rev. 595, 599 (1988). Although "the difference between accuracy, validity, and reliability may be such that each is distinct from the other by no more than a hen's kick," Starrs, *Frye* v. *United States* Restructured and Revitalized: A Proposal to Amend Federal Evidence Rule 702, 26 Jurimetrics J. 249, 256 (1986), our reference here is to *evidentiary* reliability—that is, trustworthiness. Cf., *e. g.,* Advisory Committee's Notes on Fed. Rule Evid. 602 (" '[T]he rule requiring that a witness who testifies to a fact which can be perceived by the senses must have had an opportunity to observe, and must have actually observed the fact' is a 'most pervasive manifestation' of the common law insistence upon 'the most reliable sources of information.' " (citation omitted)); Advisory Committee's Notes on Art. VIII of the Rules of Evidence (hearsay exceptions will be recognized only "under circumstances supposed to furnish guarantees of trustworthiness"). In a case involving scientific evidence, *evidentiary reliability* will be based upon *scientific validity.*

10. Rule 104(a) provides:

"Preliminary questions concerning the qualification of a person to be a witness, the existence of a privilege, or the admissibility of evidence shall be determined by the court, subject to the provisions of subdivision (b) [pertaining to conditional admissions]. In making its determination it is not bound by the rules of evidence except those with respect to privileges." These matters should be established by a preponderance of proof. See *Bourjaily v. United States,* 483 U.S. 171, 175–176 (1987).

11. Although the *Frye* decision itself focused exclusively on "novel" scientific techniques, we do not read the requirements of Rule 702 to apply specially or exclusively to unconventional evidence. Of course, well established propositions are less likely to be challenged than those that are novel, and they are more handily defended. Indeed, theories that are so firmly established as to have attained the status of scientific law, such as the laws of thermodynamics, properly are subject to judicial notice under Fed. Rule Evid. 201.

12. A number of authorities have presented variations on the reliability approach, each with its own slightly different set of factors. See, *e. g.,*

Downing, 753 F.2d 1238–1239 (on which our discussion draws in part); 3 Weinstein & Berger 702[03], pp. 702–41 to 702–42 (on which the *Downing* court in turn partially relied); McCormick, Scientific Evidence: Defining a New Approach to Admissibility, 67 Iowa L. Rev. 879, 911–912 (1982); and Symposium on Science and the Rules of Evidence, 99 F.R.D. 187, 231 (1983) (statement by Margaret Berger). To the extent that they focus on the reliability of evidence as ensured by the scientific validity of its underlying principles, all these versions may well have merit, although we express no opinion regarding any of their particular details.

13. This is not to say that judicial interpretation, as opposed to adjudicative fact-finding, does not share basic characteristics of the scientific endeavor: "The work of a judge is in one sense enduring and in another ephemeral. . . . In the endless process of testing and retesting, there is a constant rejection of the dross and a constant retention of whatever is pure and sound and fine." B. Cardozo, The Nature of the Judicial Process 178, 179 (1921).

Chief Justice REHNQUIST, with whom Justice STEVENS joins, concurring in part and dissenting in part.

The petition for certiorari in this case presents two questions: first, whether the rule of *Frye* v. *United States,* 54 App. D. C. 46, 293 F. 1013 (1923), remains good law after the enactment of the Federal Rules of Evidence; and second, if *Frye* remains valid, whether it requires expert scientific testimony to have been subjected to a peer review process in order to be admissible. The Court concludes, correctly in my view, that the *Frye* rule did not survive the enactment of the Federal Rules of Evidence, and I therefore join Parts I and II-A of its opinion. The second question presented in the petition for certiorari necessarily is mooted by this holding, but the Court nonetheless proceeds to construe Rules 702 and 703 very much in the abstract, and then offers some "general observations." *Ante,* at 12.

"General observations" by this Court customarily carry great weight with lower federal courts, but the ones offered here suffer from the flaw common to most such observations—they are not applied to deciding whether or not particular testimony was or was not admissible, and therefore they tend to be not only general, but vague and abstract. This is particularly unfortunate in a case such as this, where the ultimate legal question depends on an appreciation of one or more bodies of knowledge not judicially noticeable, and subject to different interpretations in the briefs of the parties and their *amici*. Twenty two *amicus* briefs have been filed in the case, and indeed the Court's opinion contains no less than 37 citations to *amicus* briefs and other secondary sources.

The various briefs filed in this case are markedly different from typical briefs, in that large parts of them do not deal with decided cases or statutory language—the sort of material we customarily interpret. Instead, they deal with definitions of scientific knowledge, scientific method, scientific validity, and peer review—in short, matters far afield from the expertise of judges. This is not to say that such materials are not useful or even necessary in deciding how Rule 703 should be applied; but it is to say that the unusual subject matter should cause us to proceed with great caution in deciding more than we have to, because our reach can so easily exceed our grasp.

But even if it were desirable to make "general observations" not necessary to decide the questions presented, I cannot subscribe to some of the observations made by the Court. In Part II-B, the Court concludes that reliability and relevancy are the touchstones of the admissibility of expert testimony. *Ante,* at 9. Federal Rule of Evidence 402 provides, as the Court points out, that "[e]vidence which is not relevant is not admissible." But there is no similar reference in the Rule to "reliability." The Court constructs its argument by parsing the language "[i]f scientific, technical, or other specialized knowledge will assist the trier of fact to understand the evidence or to determine a fact in issue . . . an expert . . . may testify thereto . . . ." Fed. Rule Evid. 702. It stresses that the subject of the expert's testimony must be "scientific . . . knowledge," and points out that "scientific" "implies a grounding in the methods and procedures of science," and that the word "knowledge" "connotes more than subjective belief or unsupported speculation." *Ante,* at 9. From this it concludes that "scientific knowledge" must be "derived by the scientific method." *Ante,* at 10. Proposed testimony, we are told, must be supported by "appropriate validation." *Ante,* at 10. Indeed, in footnote 9, the Court decides that "[i]n a case involving scientific evidence, *evidentiary reliability* will be based upon *scientific validity.*" *Ante,* at 10, n. 9 (emphasis in original).

Questions arise simply from reading this part of the Court's opinion, and countless more *questions* will surely arise when hundreds of district judges try to apply its teaching to particular offers of expert testimony. Does all of this *dicta* apply to an expert seeking to testify on the basis of "technical or other specialized knowledge"—the other types of expert knowledge to which Rule 702 applies—or are the "general observations" limited only to "scientific knowledge"? What is the difference between scientific knowledge and technical knowledge; does Rule 702 actually contemplate that the phrase "scientific, technical, or other specialized knowledge" be broken down into numerous subspecies of expertise, or did its authors simply pick general descriptive language covering the sort of expert testimony which courts have customarily received? The Court speaks of its confidence that federal judges can make a "preliminary assessment of whether the reasoning or methodology underlying the testimony is scientifically valid and of whether that reasoning or methodology properly can be applied to the facts in issue." *Ante,* at 12. The Court then states that a "key question" to be answered in deciding whether something is "scientific knowledge" "will be whether it can be (and has been) tested." *Ante,* at 12. Following this sentence are three quotations from treatises, which speak not only of empirical testing, but one of which states that "the criterion of the scientific status of a theory is its falsifiability, or refutability, or testability," *ante,* pp. 12–13.

I defer to no one in my confidence in federal judges; but I am at a loss to know what is meant when it is said that the scientific status of a theory depends on its "falsifiability," and I suspect some of them will be, too.

I do not doubt that Rule 702 confides to the judge some gatekeeping responsibility in deciding questions of the admissibility of proffered expert testimony. But I do not think it imposes on them either the obligation or the authority to become amateur scientists in order to perform that role. I think the Court would be far better advised in this case to decide only the questions presented, and to leave the further development of this important area of the law to future cases.

Appendix B: Kumho Tire Company, Ltd. v. Patrick Carmichael 526 U.S. 137 (1999)

Justice BREYER delivered the opinion of the Court.

In *Daubert* v. *Merrell Dow Pharmaceuticals, Inc.,* 509 U. S. 579 (1993), this Court focused upon the admissibility of scientific expert testimony. It pointed out that such testimony is admissible only if it is both relevant and reliable. And it held that the Federal Rules of Evidence "assign to the trial judge the task of ensuring that an expert's testimony both rests on a reliable foundation and is relevant to the task at hand." *Id.,* at 597. The Court also discussed certain more specific factors, such as testing, peer review, error rates, and "acceptability" in the relevant scientific community, some or all of which might prove helpful in determining the reliability of a particular scientific "theory or technique." *Id.,* at 593–594.

This case requires us to decide how *Daubert* applies to the testimony of engineers and other experts who are not scientists. We conclude that *Daubert's* general holding—setting forth the trial judge's general "gatekeeping" obligation—applies not only to testimony based on "scientific" knowledge, but also to testimony based on "technical" and "other specialized" knowledge. See Fed. Rule Evid. 702. We also conclude that a trial court *may* consider one or more of the more specific factors that *Daubert* mentioned when doing so will help determine that testimony's reliability. But, as the Court stated in *Daubert,* the test of reliability is "flexible," and *Daubert's* list of specific factors neither necessarily nor exclusively applies to all experts or in every case. Rather, the law grants a district court the same broad latitude when it decides *how* to determine reliability as it enjoys in respect to its ultimate reliability determination. See *General Electric Co.* v. *Joiner,* 522 U. S. 136, 143 (1997) (courts of appeals are to apply "abuse of discretion" standard when reviewing district court's reliability determination). Applying these standards, we determine that the District Court's decision in this case—not to admit certain expert testimony—was within its discretion and therefore lawful.

I.

On July 6, 1993, the right rear tire of a minivan driven by Patrick Carmichael blew out. In the accident that followed, one of the passengers died, and others were severely injured. In October 1993, the Carmichaels brought this diversity suit against the tire's maker and its distributor, whom we refer to collectively as Kumho Tire, claiming that the tire was defective. The plaintiffs rested their case in significant part upon deposition testimony provided by an expert in tire failure analysis, Dennis Carlson, Jr., who intended to testify in support of their conclusion.

Carlson's depositions relied upon certain features of tire technology that are not in dispute. A steel-belted radial tire like the Carmichaels' is made up of a "carcass" containing many layers of flexible cords, called "plies," along which (between the cords and the outer tread) are laid steel strips called "belts." Steel wire loops, called "beads," hold the cords together at the plies' bottom edges. An outer layer, called the "tread," encases the carcass, and the entire tire is bound together in rubber, through the application of heat and various chemicals. See generally, *e.g.,* J. Dixon, Tires, Suspension and Handling 68–72 (2d ed. 1996). The bead of the tire sits upon a "bead seat," which is part of the wheel assembly. That assembly contains a "rim flange," which extends over the bead and rests against the side of the tire. See M. Mavrigian, Performance Wheels & Tires 81, 83 (1998) (illustrations).

Carlson's testimony also accepted certain background facts about the tire in question. He assumed that before the blowout the tire had traveled far. (The tire was made in 1988 and had been installed some time before the Carmichaels bought the used minivan in March 1993; the Carmichaels had driven the van approximately 7,000 additional miles in the two months they had owned it.) Carlson noted that the tire's tread depth, which was 11/32 of an inch when new, App. 242, had been worn down to depths that ranged from 3/32 of an inch along some parts of the tire, to nothing at all along others. *Id.,* at 287. He conceded that the tire tread had at least two punctures which had been inadequately repaired. *Id.,* at 258–261, 322.

Despite the tire's age and history, Carlson concluded that a defect in its manufacture or design caused the blow-out. He rested this conclusion in part upon three premises which, for present purposes, we must assume are not in dispute: First, a tire's carcass should stay bound to the inner side of the tread for a significant period of time after its tread depth has worn away. *Id.,* at 208–209. Second, the tread of the tire at issue had separated from its inner steel-belted carcass prior to the accident. *Id.,* at 336. Third, this "separation" caused the blowout. *Ibid.*

Carlson's conclusion that a defect caused the separation, however, rested upon certain other propositions, several of which the defendants strongly dispute. First, Carlson said that if a separation is *not* caused by a certain kind of tire misuse called "overdeflection" (which consists of underinflating the tire or causing it to carry too much weight, thereby generating heat that can undo the chemical tread/carcass bond), then, ordinarily, its cause is a tire defect. *Id.,* at 193–195, 277–278. Second, he said that if a tire has been subject to sufficient overdeflection to cause a separation, it should reveal certain physical symptoms. These symptoms include (a) tread wear on the tire's shoulder that is greater than the tread wear along the tire's center, *id.,* at 211; (b) signs of a "bead groove," where the beads have been pushed too hard against the bead seat on the inside of the tire's rim, *id.,* at 196–197; (c) sidewalls of the tire with physical signs of deterioration, such as discoloration, *id.,* at 212; and/or (d) marks on the tire's rim flange, *id.,* at 219–220. Third, Carlson said that where he does not find *at least two* of the four physical signs just mentioned (and presumably where there is no reason to suspect a less common cause of separation), he concludes that a manufacturing or design defect caused the separation. *Id.,* at 223–224.

Carlson added that he had inspected the tire in question. He conceded that the tire to a limited degree showed greater wear on the shoulder than in the center, some signs of "bead groove," some discoloration, a few marks on the rim flange, and inadequately filled puncture holes (which can also cause heat that might lead to separation). *Id.,* at 256–257, 258–261, 277, 303–304, 308. But, in each instance, he testified that the symptoms were not significant, and he explained why he believed that they did not reveal overdeflection. For example, the extra shoulder wear, he said, appeared primarily on one shoulder, whereas an overdeflected tire would reveal equally abnormal wear on both shoulders. *Id.,* at 277. Carlson concluded that the tire did not bear at least two of the four overdeflection symptoms, nor was there any less obvious cause of separation; and since neither overdeflection nor the punctures caused the blowout, a defect must have done so.

Kumho Tire moved the District Court to exclude Carlson's testimony on the ground that his methodology failed Rule 702's reliability requirement. The court agreed with Kumho that it should act as a *Daubert*-type reliability "gatekeeper," even though one might consider Carlson's testimony as "technical," rather than "scientific." See *Carmichael* v. *Samyang Tires, Inc.,* 923 F. Supp. 1514, 1521–1522 (SD Ala. 1996). The court then examined Carlson's methodology in light of the reliability-related factors that *Daubert* mentioned, such as a theory's testability, whether it "has been a subject of peer review or publication," the "known or potential rate of error," and the "degree of acceptance . . . within the relevant scientific community." 923 F. Supp., at 1520 (citing *Daubert,* 509 U. S., at 592–594). The District Court found that all those factors argued against the reliability of Carlson's methods, and it granted the motion to exclude the testimony (as well as the defendants' accompanying motion for summary judgment).

The plaintiffs, arguing that the court's application of the *Daubert* factors was too "inflexible," asked for reconsideration. And the Court granted that motion. *Carmichael* v. *Samyang Tires, Inc.*, Civ. Action No. 93-0860-CB-S (SD Ala., June 5, 1996), App. to Pet. for Cert. 1c. After reconsidering the matter, the court agreed with the plaintiffs that *Daubert* should be applied flexibly, that its four factors were simply illustrative, and that other factors could argue in favor of admissibility. It conceded that there may be widespread acceptance of a "visual-inspection method" for some relevant purposes. But the court found insufficient indications of the reliability of

> "the component of Carlson's tire failure analysis which most concerned the Court, namely, the methodology employed by the expert in analyzing the data obtained in the visual inspection, and the scientific basis, if any, for such an analysis." *Id.,* at 6c.

It consequently affirmed its earlier order declaring Carlson's testimony inadmissible and granting the defendants' motion for summary judgment.

The Eleventh Circuit reversed. See *Carmichael* v. *Samyang Tire, Inc.*, 131 F.3d 1433 (1997). It "review[ed] ... *de novo*" the "district court's legal decision to apply *Daubert.*" *Id.,* at 1435. It noted that "the Supreme Court in *Daubert* explicitly limited its holding to cover only the 'scientific context,'" adding that "a *Daubert* analysis" applies only where an expert relies "on the application of scientific principles," rather than "on skill- or experience-based observation." *Id.,* at 1435–1436. It concluded that Carlson's testimony, which it viewed as relying on experience, "falls outside the scope of *Daubert,*" that "the district court erred as a matter of law by applying *Daubert* in this case," and that the case must be remanded for further (non-*Daubert*-type) consideration under Rule 702. *Id.,* at 1436.

Kumho Tire petitioned for certiorari, asking us to determine whether a trial court "may" consider *Daubert's* specific "factors" when determining the "admissibility of an engineering expert's testimony." Pet. for Cert. i. We granted certiorari in light of uncertainty among the lower courts about whether, or how, *Daubert* applies to expert testimony that might be characterized as based not upon "scientific" knowledge, but rather upon "technical" or "other specialized" knowledge. Fed. Rule Evid. 702; compare, *e.g.,* *Watkins* v. *Telsmith, Inc.,* 121 F. 3d 984, 990–991 (CA5 1997), with, *e.g., Compton* v. *Subaru of America, Inc.,* 82 F. 3d 1513, 1518–1519 (CA10), cert. denied, 519 U. S. 1042 (1996).

II.
A.

In *Daubert,* this Court held that Federal Rule of Evidence 702 imposes a special obligation upon a trial judge to "ensure that any and all scientific testimony . . . is not only relevant, but reliable." 509 U. S., at 589. The initial question before us is whether this basic gatekeeping obligation applies only to "scientific" testimony or to all expert testimony. We, like the parties, believe that it applies to all expert testimony. See Brief for Petitioners 19; Brief for Respondents 17.

For one thing, Rule 702 itself says:

> "If scientific, technical, or other specialized knowledge will assist the trier of fact to understand the evidence or to determine a fact in issue, a witness qualified as an expert by knowledge, skill, experience, training, or education, may testify thereto in the form of an opinion or otherwise."

This language makes no relevant distinction between "scientific" knowledge and "technical" or "other specialized" knowledge. It makes clear that any such knowledge might become the subject of expert testimony. In *Daubert,* the Court specified that it is the Rule's word "knowledge," not the words (like "scientific") that modify that word, that "establishes a standard of evidentiary reliability." 509 U. S., at 589–590. Hence, as a matter of language, the Rule applies its reliability standard to all "scientific," "technical," or "other specialized" matters within its scope. We concede that the Court in *Daubert* referred only to "scientific" knowledge. But as the Court there said, it referred to "scientific" testimony "because that [wa]s the nature of the expertise" at issue. *Id.,* at 590, n. 8.

Neither is the evidentiary rationale that underlay the Court's basic *Daubert* "gatekeeping" determination limited to "scientific" knowledge. *Daubert* pointed out that Federal Rules 702 and 703 grant expert witnesses testimonial latitude unavailable to other witnesses on the "assumption that the expert's opinion will have a reliable basis in the knowledge and experience of his discipline." *Id.,* at 592 (pointing out that experts may testify to opinions, including those that are not based on firsthand knowledge or observation). The Rules grant that latitude to all experts, not just to "scientific" ones.

Finally, it would prove difficult, if not impossible, for judges to administer evidentiary rules under which a gatekeeping obligation depended upon a distinction between "scientific" knowledge and "technical" or "other specialized" knowledge. There is no clear line that divides the one from the others. Disciplines such as engineering rest upon scientific knowledge. Pure scientific theory itself may depend for its development upon observation and properly engineered machinery. And conceptual efforts to distinguish the two are unlikely to produce clear legal lines capable of application in particular cases. Cf. Brief for National Academy of Engineering as *Amicus Curiae* 9 (scientist seeks to understand nature while the engineer seeks nature's modification); Brief for Rubber Manufacturers Association as *Amicus Curiae* 14–16 (engineering, as an "applied science," relies on "scientific reasoning and methodology"); Brief for John Allen et al. as *Amici Curiae* 6 (engineering relies upon "scientific knowledge and methods").

Neither is there a convincing need to make such distinctions. Experts of all kinds tie observations to conclusions through the use of what Judge Learned Hand called "general truths derived from ... specialized experience." Hand, Historical and Practical Considerations Regarding Expert Testimony, 15 Harv. L. Rev. 40, 54 (1901). And whether the specific expert testimony focuses upon specialized observations, the specialized translation of those observations into theory, a specialized theory itself, or the application of such a theory in a particular case, the expert's testimony often will rest "upon an experience confessedly foreign in kind to [the jury's] own." *Ibid.* The trial judge's effort to assure that the specialized testimony is reliable and relevant can help the jury evaluate that foreign experience, whether the testimony reflects scientific, technical, or other specialized knowledge.

We conclude that *Daubert's* general principles apply to the expert matters described in Rule 702. The Rule, in respect to all such matters, "establishes a standard of evidentiary reliability." 509 U. S., at 590, 113 S. Ct. 2786. It "requires a valid . . . connection to the pertinent inquiry as a precondition to admissibility." *Id.,* at 592. And where such testimony's factual basis, data, principles, methods, or their application are called sufficiently into question, see Part III, *infra,* the trial judge must determine whether the testimony has "a reliable basis in the knowledge and experience of [the relevant] discipline." 509 U. S., at 592, 13 S. Ct. 2786.

B.

The petitioners ask more specifically whether a trial judge determining the "admissibility of an engineering expert's testimony" *may* consider several more specific factors that *Daubert* said might "bear on" a judge's gate-keeping determination. These factors include:

— Whether a "theory or technique . . . can be (and has been) tested";
— Whether it "has been subjected to peer review and publication";
— Whether, in respect to a particular technique, there is a high "known or potential rate of error" and whether there are "standards controlling the technique's operation"; and
— Whether the theory or technique enjoys "general acceptance" within a "relevant scientific community." 509 U. S., at 592–594, 113 S. Ct. 2786.

Emphasizing the word "may" in the question, we answer that question yes.

Engineering testimony rests upon scientific foundations, the reliability of which will be at issue in some cases. See, *e.g.,* Brief for Stephen Bobo et al. as *Amici Curiae* 23 (stressing the scientific bases of engineering disciplines). In other cases, the relevant reliability concerns may focus upon personal knowledge or experience. As the Solicitor General points out, there are many different kinds of experts, and many different kinds of expertise. See Brief for United States as *Amicus Curiae* 18–19, and n. 5 (citing cases involving experts in drug terms, handwriting analysis, criminal *modus operandi,* land valuation, agricultural practices, railroad procedures, attorney's fee valuation, and others). Our emphasis on the word "may" thus reflects *Daubert's* description of the Rule 702 inquiry as "a flexible one." 509 U.S., at 594, 113 S. Ct. 2786. *Daubert* makes clear that the factors it mentions do *not* constitute a "definitive checklist or test." *Id.,* at 593. And *Daubert* adds that the gatekeeping inquiry must be " 'tied to the facts' " of a particular "case." *Id.,* at 591 (quoting *United States* v. *Downing,* 753 F.2d 1224, 1242 (CA3 1985)). We agree with the Solicitor General that "[t]he factors identified in *Daubert* may or may not be pertinent in assessing reliability, depending on the nature of the issue, the expert's particular expertise, and the subject of his testimony." Brief for United States as *Amicus Curiae* 19. The conclusion, in our view, is that we can neither rule out, nor rule in, for all cases and for all time the applicability of the factors mentioned in *Daubert,* nor can we now do so for subsets of cases categorized by category of expert or by kind of evidence. Too much depends upon the particular circumstances of the particular case at issue.

Daubert itself is not to the contrary. It made clear that its list of factors was meant to be helpful, not definitive. Indeed, those factors do not all necessarily apply even in every instance in which the reliability of scientific testimony is challenged. It might not be surprising in a particular case, for example, that a claim made by a scientific witness has never been the subject of peer review, for the particular application at issue may never previously have interested any scientist. Nor, on the other hand, does the presence of *Daubert's* general acceptance factor help show that an expert's testimony is reliable where the discipline itself lacks reliability, as, for example, do theories grounded in any so-called generally accepted principles of astrology or necromancy.

At the same time, and contrary to the Court of Appeals' view, some of *Daubert's* questions can help to evaluate the reliability even of experience-based testimony. In certain cases, it will be appropriate for the trial judge to ask, for example, how often an engineering expert's experience-based methodology has produced erroneous results, or whether such a method is generally accepted in the relevant engineering community. Likewise, it will at times be useful to ask even of a witness whose expertise is based purely on experience, say, a perfume tester able to distinguish among 140 odors at a sniff, whether his preparation is of a kind that others in the field would recognize as acceptable.

We must therefore disagree with the Eleventh Circuit's holding that a trial judge may ask questions of the sort *Daubert* mentioned only where an expert "relies on the application of scientific principles," but not where an expert relies "on skill- or experience-based observation." 131 F. 3d, at 1435. We do not believe that Rule 702 creates a schematism that segregates expertise by type while mapping certain kinds of questions to certain kinds of experts. Life and the legal cases that it generates are too complex to warrant so definitive a match.

To say this is not to deny the importance of *Daubert's* gatekeeping requirement. The objective of that requirement is to ensure the reliability and relevancy of expert testimony. It is to make certain that an expert, whether basing testimony upon professional studies or personal experience, employs in the courtroom the same level of intellectual rigor that characterizes the practice of an expert in the relevant field. Nor do we deny that, as stated in *Daubert,* the particular questions that it mentioned will often be appropriate for use in determining the reliability of challenged expert testimony. Rather, we conclude that the trial judge must have considerable leeway in deciding in a particular case how to go about determining whether particular expert testimony is reliable. That is to say, a trial court should consider the specific factors identified in *Daubert* where they are reasonable measures of the reliability of expert testimony.

C.

The trial court must have the same kind of latitude in deciding *how* to test an expert's reliability, and to decide whether or when special briefing or other proceedings are needed to investigate reliability, as it enjoys when it decides *whether* that expert's relevant testimony is reliable. Our opinion in *Joiner* makes clear that a court of appeals is to apply an abuse-of-discretion standard when it "review[s] a trial court's decision to admit or exclude expert testimony." 522 U. S., at 138–139. That standard applies as much to the trial court's decisions about how to determine reliability as to its ultimate conclusion. Otherwise, the trial judge would lack the discretionary authority needed both to avoid unnecessary "reliability" proceedings in ordinary cases where the reliability of an expert's methods is properly taken for granted, and to require appropriate proceedings in the less usual or more complex cases where cause for questioning the expert's reliability arises. Indeed, the Rules seek to avoid "unjustifiable expense and delay" as part of their search for "truth" and the "jus[t] determin[ation]" of proceedings. Fed. Rule Evid. 102. Thus, whether *Daubert's* specific factors are, or are not, reasonable measures of reliability in a particular case is a matter that the law grants the trial judge broad latitude to determine. See *Joiner, supra,* at 143. And the Eleventh Circuit erred insofar as it held to the contrary.

III.

We further explain the way in which a trial judge "may" consider *Daubert's* factors by applying these considerations to the case at hand, a matter that has been briefed exhaustively by the parties and their 19 *amici.* The District Court did not doubt Carlson's qualifications, which included a masters degree in mechanical engineering, 10 years' work at Michelin America, Inc., and testimony as a tire failure consultant in other tort cases. Rather, it excluded the testimony because, despite those qualifications, it initially doubted, and then found unreliable, "the methodology employed by the expert in analyzing the data obtained in the visual inspection, and the scientific basis, if any, for such an analysis." Civ. Action No. 93-0860-CB-S (SD Ala., June 5, 1996), App. to Pet. for Cert. 6c. After examining the transcript in "some detail," 923 F. Supp., at 1518–519, n. 4, and after considering respondents' defense of Carlson's methodology, the District Court determined that Carlson's testimony was not reliable. It fell outside the range where experts might reasonably differ, and where the jury must decide among the conflicting views of different experts, even though the evidence is "shaky." *Daubert,* 509 U. S., at 596. In our view, the doubts that triggered the District Court's initial inquiry here were reasonable, as was the court's ultimate conclusion.

For one thing, and contrary to respondents' suggestion, the specific issue before the court was not the reasonableness *in general* of a tire expert's use of a visual and tactile inspection to determine whether overdeflection had caused the tire's tread to separate from its steel-belted carcass. Rather, it was the reasonableness of using such an approach, along with Carlson's particular method of analyzing the data thereby obtained, to draw a conclusion regarding *the particular matter to which the expert testimony was directly relevant.* That matter concerned the likelihood that a defect in the tire at issue caused its tread to separate from its carcass. The tire in question, the expert conceded, had traveled far enough so that some of the tread had been worn bald; it should have been taken out of service; it had been repaired (inadequately) for punctures; and it bore some of the very marks that the expert said indicated, not a defect, but abuse through overdeflection. See *supra,* at 3–5; App. 293–294. The relevant issue was whether the expert could reliably determine the cause of *this* tire's separation.

Nor was the basis for Carlson's conclusion simply the general theory that, in the absence of evidence of abuse, a defect will normally have caused a tire's separation. Rather, the expert employed a more specific theory to establish the existence (or absence) of such abuse. Carlson testified precisely that in the absence of *at least two* of four signs of abuse (proportionately greater tread wear on the shoulder; signs of grooves caused by the beads; discolored sidewalls; marks on the rim flange) he concludes that a defect caused the separation. And his analysis depended upon acceptance of a further implicit proposition, namely, that his visual and tactile inspection could determine that the tire before him had not been abused despite some evidence of the presence of the very signs for which he looked (and two punctures).

For another thing, the transcripts of Carlson's depositions support both the trial court's initial uncertainty and its final conclusion. Those transcripts cast considerable doubt upon the reliability of both the explicit theory (about the need for two signs of abuse) and the implicit proposition (about the significance of visual inspection in this case). Among other things, the expert could not say whether the tire had traveled more than 10, or 20, or 30, or 40, or 50 thousand miles, adding that 6,000 miles was "about how far" he could "say with any certainty." *Id.,* at 265. The court could reasonably have wondered about the reliability of a method of visual and tactile inspection sufficiently precise to ascertain with some certainty the abuse-related significance of minute shoulder/center relative tread wear differences, but insufficiently precise to tell "with any certainty" from the tread wear whether a tire had traveled less than 10,000 or more than 50,000 miles. And these concerns might have been augmented by Carlson's repeated reliance on the "subjective[ness]" of his mode of analysis in response to questions seeking specific information regarding how he could differentiate between a tire that actually had been overdeflected and a tire that merely looked as though it had been. *Id.,* at 222, 224–225, 285–286. They would have been further augmented by the fact that Carlson said he had inspected the tire itself for the first time the morning of his first deposition, and then only for a few hours. (His initial conclusions were based on photographs.) *Id.,* at 180.

Moreover, prior to his first deposition, Carlson had issued a signed report in which he concluded that the tire had "not been . . . overloaded or underinflated," not because of the absence of "two of four" signs of abuse, but simply because "the rim flange impressions . . . were normal." *Id.,* at 335–336. That report also said that the "tread depth remaining was 3/32 inch," *id.,* at 336, though the opposing expert's (apparently undisputed) measurements indicate that the tread depth taken at various positions around the tire actually ranged from 5/32 of an inch to 4/32 of an inch, with the tire apparently showing greater wear along *both* shoulders than along the center, *id.,* at 432–433.

Further, in respect to one sign of abuse, bead grooving, the expert seemed to deny the sufficiency of his own simple visual-inspection methodology. He testified that most tires have some bead groove pattern, that where there is reason to suspect an abnormal bead groove he would ideally "look at a lot of [similar] tires" to know the grooving's significance, and that he had not looked at many tires similar to the one at issue. *Id.,* at 212–213, 214, 217.

Finally, the court, after looking for a defense of Carlson's methodology as applied in these circumstances, found no convincing defense. Rather, it found (1) that "none" of the *Daubert* factors, including that of "general acceptance" in the relevant expert community, indicated that Carlson's testimony was reliable, 923 F. Supp., at 1521; (2) that its own analysis "revealed no countervailing factors operating in favor of admissibility which could outweigh those identified in *Daubert,*" App. to Pet. for Cert. 4c; and (3) that the "parties identified no such factors in their briefs," *ibid.* For these three reasons *taken together,* it concluded that Carlson's testimony was unreliable.

Respondents now argue to us, as they did to the District Court, that a method of tire failure analysis that employs a visual/tactile inspection is a reliable method, and they point both to its use by other experts and to Carlson's long experience working for Michelin as sufficient indication that that is so. But no one denies that an expert might draw a conclusion from a set of observations based on extensive and specialized experience. Nor does anyone deny that, as a general matter, tire abuse may often be identified by qualified experts through visual or tactile inspection of the tire. See Affidavit of H. R. Baumgardner 1–2, cited in Brief for National Academy of Forensic Engineers as *Amici Curiae* 16 (Tire engineers rely on visual examination and process of elimination to analyze experimental test tires). As we said before, *supra,* at 14, the question before the trial court was specific, not general. The trial court had to decide whether this particular expert had sufficient specialized knowledge to assist the jurors "in deciding the particular issues in the case." 4 J. McLaughlin, Weinstein's Federal Evidence ¶ 702.05[1], p. 702–33 (2d ed. 1998); see also Advisory Committee's Note on Proposed Fed. Rule Evid. 702, Preliminary Draft of Proposed Amendments to the Federal Rules of Civil Procedure and Evidence: Request for Comment 126 (1998) (stressing that district courts must "scrutinize" whether the "principles and methods" employed by an expert "have been properly applied to the facts of the case").

The particular issue in this case concerned the use of Carlson's two-factor test and his related use of visual/tactile inspection to draw conclusions on the basis of what seemed small observational differences. We have found no indication in the record that other experts in the industry use Carlson's two-factor test or that tire experts such as Carlson normally make the very fine distinctions about, say, the symmetry of comparatively greater shoulder tread wear that were necessary, on Carlson's own theory, to support his conclusions. Nor, despite the prevalence of tire testing, does anyone refer to any articles or papers that validate Carlson's approach. Compare Bobo, Tire Flaws and Separations, in Mechanics of Pneumatic Tires 636–637 (S. Clark ed. 1981); C. Schnuth et al., Compression Grooving and Rim Flange Abrasion as Indicators of Over-Deflected Operating Conditions in Tires, presented to Rubber Division of the American Chemical Society, Oct. 21–24, 1997; J. Walter & R. Kiminecz, Bead Contact Pressure Measurements at the Tire-Rim Interface, presented to Society of Automotive Engineers, Feb. 24–28, 1975. Indeed, no one has argued that Carlson himself, were he still working for Michelin, would have concluded in a report to his employer that a similar tire was similarly defective on grounds identical to those upon which he rested his conclusion here. Of course, Carlson himself claimed that his method was accurate, but, as we pointed out in *Joiner,* "nothing in either *Daubert* or the Federal Rules of Evidence requires a district court to admit opinion evidence that is connected to existing data only by the *ipse dixit* of the expert." 522 U. S., at 146.

Respondents additionally argue that the District Court too rigidly applied *Daubert's* criteria. They read its opinion to hold that a failure to satisfy any one of those criteria automatically renders expert testimony inadmissible. The District Court's initial opinion might have been vulnerable to a form of this argument. There, the court, after rejecting respondents' claim that Carlson's testimony was "exempted from *Daubert*-style scrutiny" because it was "technical analysis" rather than "scientific evidence," simply added that "none of the four admissibility criteria outlined by the *Daubert* court are satisfied." 923 F. Supp., at 1522. Subsequently, however, the court granted respondents' motion for reconsideration. It then explicitly recognized that the relevant reliability inquiry "should be 'flexible,'" that its "'overarching subject [should be] . . . validity' and reliability," and that "*Daubert* was intended neither to be exhaustive nor to apply in every case." App. to Pet. for Cert. 4c (quoting *Daubert,* 509 U. S., at 594–595). And the court ultimately based its decision upon Carlson's failure to satisfy either *Daubert's* factors *or any other* set of reasonable reliability criteria. In light of the record as developed by the parties, that conclusion was within the District Court's lawful discretion.

In sum, Rule 702 grants the district judge the discretionary authority, reviewable for its abuse, to determine reliability in light of the particular facts and circumstances of the particular case. The District Court did not abuse its discretionary authority in this case. Hence, the judgment of the Court of Appeals is *Reversed.*

Justice SCALIA, with whom Justice O'CONNOR and Justice THOMAS join, concurring.

I join the opinion of the Court, which makes clear that the discretion it endorses—trial-court discretion in choosing the manner of testing expert reliability—is not discretion to abandon the gatekeeping function. I think it worth adding that it is not discretion to perform the function inadequately. Rather, it is discretion to choose among reasonable means of excluding expertise that is *fausse* and science that is junky. Though, as the Court makes clear today, the Daubert factors are not holy writ, in a particular case the failure to apply one or another of them may be unreasonable, and hence an abuse of discretion.

Justice STEVENS, concurring in part and dissenting in part.

The only question that we granted certiorari to decide is whether a trial judge "[m]ay . . . consider the four factors set out by this Court in *Daubert* v. *Merrill Dow Pharmaceuticals, Inc.,* 509 U. S. 579 (1993), in a Rule 702 analysis of admissibility of an engineering expert's testimony." Pet. for Cert. i. That question is fully and correctly answered in Parts I and II of the Court's opinion, which I join.

Part III answers the quite different question whether the trial judge abused his discretion when he excluded the testimony of Dennis Carlson. Because a proper answer to that question requires a study of the record that can be performed more efficiently by the

Court of Appeals than by the nine Members of this Court, I would remand the case to the Eleventh Circuit to perform that task. There are, of course, exceptions to most rules, but I firmly believe that it is neither fair to litigants nor good practice for this Court to reach out to decide questions not raised by the certiorari petition. See *General Electric Co.* v. *Joiner,* 522 U. S. 136, 150–151 (1997) (*Stevens, J.,* concurring in part and dissenting in part).

Accordingly, while I do not feel qualified to disagree with the well-reasoned factual analysis in Part III of the Court's opinion, I do not join that Part, and I respectfully dissent from the Court's disposition of the case.

Appendix C: Federal Rules of Civil Procedure Rule 26. General Provisions Governing Discovery; Duty of Disclosure

(a) **Required Disclosures; Methods to Discover Additional Matter.**

    (1) *Initial Disclosures.* Except in categories of proceedings specified in Rule 26(a)(1)(E), or to the extent otherwise stipulated or directed by order, a party must, without awaiting a discovery request, provide to other parties:

        (A) the name and, if known, the address and telephone number of each individual likely to have discoverable information that the disclosing party may use to support its claims or defenses, unless solely for impeachment, identifying the subjects of the information;

(B) a copy of, or a description by category and location of, all documents, data compilations, and tangible things that are in the possession, custody, or control of the party and that the disclosing party may use to support its claims or defenses, unless solely for impeachment;

(C) a computation of any category of damages claimed by the disclosing party, making available for inspection and copying as under Rule 34 the documents or other evidentiary material, not privileged or protected from disclosure, on which such computation is based, including materials bearing on the nature and extent of injuries suffered; and

(D) for inspection and copying as under Rule 34 any insurance agreement under which any person carrying on an insurance business may be liable to satisfy part or all of a judgment which may be entered in the action or to indemnify or reimburse for payments made to satisfy the judgment.

(E) The following categories of proceedings are exempt from initial disclosure under Rule 26(a)(1):

    (i) an action for review on an administrative record;

    (ii) a petition for habeas corpus or other proceeding to challenge a criminal conviction or sentence;

    (iii) an action brought without counsel by a person in custody of the United States, a state, or a state subdivision;

    (iv) an action to enforce or quash an administrative summons or subpoena;

    (v) an action by the United States to recover benefit payments;

    (vi) an action by the United States to collect on a student loan guaranteed by the United States;

(vii)   a proceeding ancillary to proceedings in other courts; and

(viii) an action to enforce an arbitration award.

These disclosures must be made at or within 14 days after the Rule 26(f) conference unless a different time is set by stipulation or court order, or unless a party objects during the conference that initial disclosures are not appropriate in the circumstances of the action and states the objection in the Rule 26(f) discovery plan. In ruling on the objection, the court must determine what disclosures—if any—are to be made, and set the time for disclosure. Any party first served or otherwise joined after the Rule 26(f) conference must make these disclosures within 30 days after being served or joined unless a different time is set by stipulation or court order. A party must make its initial disclosures based on the information then reasonably available to it and is not excused from making its disclosures because it has not fully completed its investigation of the case or because it challenges the sufficiency of another party's disclosures or because another party has not made its disclosures.

(2)   *Disclosure of Expert Testimony.*

(A)   In addition to the disclosures required by paragraph (1), a party shall disclose to other parties the identity of any person who may be used at trial to present evidence under Rules 702, 703, or 705 of the Federal Rules of Evidence.

(B)   Except as otherwise stipulated or directed by the court, this disclosure shall, with respect to a witness who is retained or specially employed to provide expert testimony in the case or whose duties as an employee of the party regularly involve giving expert testimony, be accompanied by a written report prepared and signed by the witness. The report shall contain a complete statement of all opinions to be expressed and the basis and reasons therefor; the data or other information considered by the witness in forming the opinions; any exhibits to be used as a summary of or support for the opinions; the qualifications of the witness, including a list of all publications authored by the witness within the preceding ten years; the compensation to be paid for the study and testimony; and a listing of any other cases in which the witness has testified as an expert at trial or by deposition within the preceding four years.

(C) These disclosures shall be made at the times and in the sequence directed by the court. In the absence of other directions from the court or stipulation by the parties, the disclosures shall be made at least 90 days before the trial date or the date the case is to be ready for trial or, if the evidence is intended solely to contradict or rebut evidence on the same subject matter identified by another party under paragraph (2)(B), within 30 days after the disclosure made by the other party. The parties shall supplement these disclosures when required under subdivision (e)(1).

(3) *Pretrial Disclosures.* In addition to the disclosures required by Rule 26(a)(1) and (2), a party must provide to other parties and promptly file with the court the following information regarding the evidence that it may present at trial other than solely for impeachment:

(A) the name and, if not previously provided, the address and telephone number of each witness, separately identifying those whom the party expects to present and those whom the party may call if the need arises;

(B) the designation of those witnesses whose testimony is expected to be presented by means of a deposition and, if not taken stenographically, a transcript of the pertinent portions of the deposition testimony; and

(C) an appropriate identification of each document or other exhibit, including summaries of other evidence, separately identifying those which the party expects to offer and those which the party may offer if the need arises.

Unless otherwise directed by the court, these disclosures must be made at least 30 days before trial. Within 14 days thereafter, unless a different time is specified by the court, a party may serve and promptly file a list disclosing (i) any objections to the use under Rule 32(a) of a deposition designated by another party under Rule 26(a)(3)(B), and (ii) any objection, together with the grounds therefor, that may be made to the admissibility of materials identified under Rule 26(a)(3)(C). Objections not so disclosed, other than objections under Rules 402 and 403 of the Federal Rules of Evidence, are waived unless excused by the court for good cause.

> (4) *Form of Disclosures.*Unless the court orders otherwise, all disclosures under Rules 26(a)(1) through (3) must be made in writing, signed, and served.
>
> (5) *Methods to Discover Additional Matter.* Parties may obtain discovery by one or more of the following methods: depositions upon oral examination or written questions; written interrogatories; production of documents or things or permission to enter upon land or other property under Rule 34 or 45(a)(1)(C), for inspection and other purposes; physical and mental examinations; and requests for admission.

(b) Discovery Scope and Limits. Unless otherwise limited by order of the court in accordance with these rules, the scope of discovery is as follows:

> (1) *In General.* Parties may obtain discovery regarding any matter, not privileged, that is relevant to the claim or defense of any party, including the existence, description, nature, custody, condition, and location of any books, documents, or other tangible things and the identity and location of persons having knowledge of any discoverable matter. For good cause, the court may order discovery of any matter relevant to the subject matter involved in the action. Relevant information need not be admissible at the trial if the discovery appears reasonably calculated to lead to the discovery of admissible evidence. All discovery is subject to the limitations imposed by Rule 26(b)(2)(i), (ii), and (iii).

(2) *Limitations.* By order, the court may alter the limits in these rules on the number of depositions and interrogatories or the length of depositions under Rule 30. By order or local rule, the court may also limit the number of requests under Rule 36. The frequency or extent of use of the discovery methods otherwise permitted under these rules and by any local rule shall be limited by the court if it determines that: (i) the discovery sought is unreasonably cumulative or duplicative, or is obtainable from some other source that is more convenient, less burdensome, or less expensive; (ii) the party seeking discovery has had ample opportunity by discovery in the action to obtain the information sought; or (iii) the burden or expense of the proposed discovery outweighs its likely benefit, taking into account the needs of the case, the amount in controversy, the parties' resources, the importance of the issues at stake in the litigation, and the importance of the proposed discovery in resolving the issues. The court may act upon its own initiative after reasonable notice or pursuant to a motion under Rule 26(c).

(3) *Trial Preparation: Materials.* Subject to the provisions of subdivision (b)(4) of this rule, a party may obtain discovery of documents and tangible things otherwise discoverable under subdivision (b)(1) of this rule and prepared in anticipation of litigation or for trial by or for another party or by or for that other party's representative (including the other party's attorney, consultant, surety, indemnitor, insurer, or agent) only upon a showing that the party seeking discovery has substantial need of the materials in the preparation of the party's case and that the party is unable without undue hardship to obtain the substantial equivalent of the materials by other means. In ordering discovery of such materials when the required showing has been made, the court shall protect against disclosure of the mental impressions, conclusions, opinions, or legal theories of an attorney or other representative of a party concerning the litigation.

A party may obtain without the required showing a statement concerning the action or its subject matter previously made by that party. Upon request, a person not a party may obtain without the required showing a statement concerning the action or its subject matter previously made by that person. If the request is refused, the person may move for a court order. The provisions of Rule 37(a)(4) apply to the award of expenses incurred in relation to the motion. For purposes of this paragraph, a statement previously made is (A) a written statement signed or otherwise adopted or approved by the person making it, or (B) a stenographic, mechanical, electrical, or other recording, or a transcription thereof, which is a substantially verbatim recital of an oral statement by the person making it and contemporaneously recorded.

(4) *Trial Preparation: Experts.*

    (A) A party may depose any person who has been identified as an expert whose opinions may be presented at trial. If a report from the expert is required under subdivision (a)(2)(B), the deposition shall not be conducted until after the report is provided.

    (B) A party may, through interrogatories or by deposition, discover facts known or opinions held by an expert who has been retained or specially employed by another party in anticipation of litigation or preparation for trial and who is not expected to be called as a witness at trial, only as provided in Rule 35(b) or upon a showing of exceptional circumstances under which it is impracticable for the party seeking discovery to obtain facts or opinions on the same subject by other means.

    (C) Unless manifest injustice would result, (i) the court shall require that the party seeking discovery pay the expert a reasonable fee for time spent in responding to discovery under this subdivision; and (ii) with respect to discovery obtained under subdivision (b)(4)(B) of this rule the court shall require the party seeking discovery to pay the other party a fair portion of the fees and expenses reasonably incurred by the latter party in obtaining facts and opinions from the expert.

(5) *Claims of Privilege or Protection of Trial Preparation Materials.* When a party withholds information otherwise discoverable under these rules by claiming that it is privileged or subject to protection as trial preparation material, the party shall make the claim expressly and shall describe the nature of the documents, communications, or things not produced or disclosed in a manner that, without revealing information itself privileged or protected, will enable other parties to assess the applicability of the privilege or protection.

(c) **Protective Orders.** Upon motion by a party or by the person from whom discovery is sought, accompanied by a certification that the movant has in good faith conferred or attempted to confer with other affected parties in an effort to resolve the dispute without court action, and for good cause shown, the court in which the action is pending or alternatively, on matters relating to a deposition, the court in the district where the deposition is to be taken may make any order which justice requires to protect a party or person from annoyance, embarrassment, oppression, or undue burden or expense, including one or more of the following:

(1) that the disclosure or discovery not be had;

(2) that the disclosure or discovery may be had only on specified terms and conditions, including a designation of the time or place;

(3) that the discovery may be had only by a method of discovery other than that selected by the party seeking discovery;

(4) that certain matters not be inquired into, or that the scope of the disclosure or discovery be limited to certain matters;

(5) that discovery be conducted with no one present except persons designated by the court;

(6) that a deposition, after being sealed, be opened only by order of the court;

(7) that a trade secret or other confidential research, development, or commercial information not be revealed or be revealed only in a designated way; and

(8) that the parties simultaneously file specified documents or information enclosed in sealed envelopes to be opened as directed by the court.

If the motion for a protective order is denied in whole or in part, the court may, on such terms and conditions as are just, order that any party or other person provide or permit discovery. The provisions of Rule 37(a)(4) apply to the award of expenses incurred in relation to the motion.

(d) Timing and Sequence of Discovery. Except in categories of proceedings exempted from initial disclosure under Rule 26(a)(1)(E), or when authorized under these rules or by order or agreement of the parties, a party may not seek discovery from any source before the parties have conferred as required by Rule 26(f). Unless the court upon motion, for the convenience of parties and witnesses and in the interests of justice, orders otherwise, methods of discovery may be used in any sequence, and the fact that a party is conducting discovery, whether by deposition or otherwise, does not operate to delay any other party's discovery.

(e) Supplementation of Disclosures and Responses. A party who has made a disclosure under subdivision (a) or responded to a request for discovery with a disclosure or response is under a duty to supplement or correct the disclosure or response to include information thereafter acquired if ordered by the court or in the following circumstances:

(1) A party is under a duty to supplement at appropriate intervals its disclosures under subdivision (a) if the party learns that in some material respect the information disclosed is incomplete or incorrect and if the additional or corrective information has not otherwise been made known to the other parties during the discovery process or in writing. With respect to testimony of an expert from whom a report is required under subdivision

(a)(2)(B) the duty extends both to information contained in the report and to information provided through a deposition of the expert, and any additions or other changes to this information shall be disclosed by the time the party's disclosures under Rule 26(a)(3) are due.

(2) A party is under a duty seasonably to amend a prior response to an interrogatory, request for production, or request for admission if the party learns that the response is in some material respect incomplete or incorrect and if the additional or corrective information has not otherwise been made known to the other parties during the discovery process or in writing.

(f) Meeting of Parties; Planning for Discovery. Except in categories of proceedings exempted from initial disclosure under Rule 26(a)(1)(E) or when otherwise ordered, the parties must, as soon as practicable and in any event at least 21 days before a scheduling conference is held or a scheduling order is due under Rule 16(b), confer to consider the nature and basis of their claims and defenses and the possibilities for a prompt settlement or resolution of the case, to make or arrange for the disclosures required by Rule 26(a)(1), and to develop a proposed discovery plan that indicates the parties' views and proposals concerning:

(1) what changes should be made in the timing, form, or requirement for disclosures under Rule 26(a), including a statement as to when disclosures under Rule 26(a)(1) were made or will be made;

(2) the subjects on which discovery may be needed, when discovery should be completed, and whether discovery should be conducted in phases or be limited to or focused upon particular issues;

(3) what changes should be made in the limitations on discovery imposed under these rules or by local rule, and what other limitations should be imposed; and

(4) any other orders that should be entered by the court under Rule 26(c) or under Rule 16(b) and (c).

The attorneys of record and all unrepresented parties that have appeared in the case are jointly responsible for arranging the conference, for attempting in good faith to agree on the proposed discovery plan, and for submitting to the court within 14 days after the conference a written report outlining the plan. A court may order that the parties or attorneys attend the conference in person. If necessary to comply with its expedited schedule for Rule 16(b) conferences, a court may by local rule (i) require that the conference between the parties occur fewer than 21 days before the scheduling conference is held or a scheduling order is due under Rule 16(b), and (ii) require that the written report outlining the discovery plan be filed fewer than 14 days after the conference between the parties, or excuse the parties from submitting a written report and permit them to report orally on their discovery plan at the Rule 16(b) conference.

(g) Signing of Disclosures, Discovery Requests, Responses, and Objections.

    (1)   Every disclosure made pursuant to subdivision (a)(1) or subdivision (a)(3) shall be signed by at least one attorney of record in the attorney's individual name, whose address shall be stated. An unrepresented party shall sign the disclosure and state the party's address. The signature of the attorney or party constitutes a certification that to the best of the signer's knowledge, information, and belief, formed after a reasonable inquiry, the disclosure is complete and correct as of the time it is made.

    (2)   Every discovery request, response, or objection made by a party represented by an attorney shall be signed by at least one attorney of record in the attorney's individual name, whose address shall be stated. An unrepresented party shall sign the request, response, or objection and state the party's address. The signature of the attorney or party constitutes a certification that to the best of the signer's knowledge, information, and belief, formed after a reasonable inquiry, the request, response, or objection is:

        (A)   consistent with these rules and warranted by existing law or a good faith argument for the extension, modification, or reversal of existing law;

    (B)   not interposed for any improper purpose, such as to harass or to cause unnecessary delay or needless increase in the cost of litigation; and

    (C)   not unreasonable or unduly burdensome or expensive, given the needs of the case, the discovery already had in the case, the amount in controversy, and the importance of the issues at stake in the litigation.

If a request, response, or objection is not signed, it shall be stricken unless it is signed promptly after the omission is called to the attention of the party making the request, response, or objection, and a party shall not be obligated to take any action with respect to it until it is signed.

    (3)   If without substantial justification a certification is made in violation of the rule, the court, upon motion or upon its own initiative, shall impose upon the person who made the certification, the party on whose behalf the disclosure, request, response, or objection is made, or both, an appropriate sanction, which may include an order to pay the amount of the reasonable expenses incurred because of the violation, including a reasonable attorney's fee.

Appendix D: Federal Rules of Evidence

Rule 701. Opinion Testimony by Lay Witnesses

If the witness is not testifying as an expert, the witness' testimony in the form of opinions or inferences is limited to those opinions or inferences which are (a) rationally based on the perception of the witness, and (b) helpful to a clear understanding of the witness' testimony or the determination of a fact in issue, and (c) not based on scientific, technical, or other specialized knowledge within the scope of Rule 702.

Rule 702. Testimony by Experts

If scientific, technical, or other specialized knowledge will assist the trier of fact to understand the evidence or to determine a fact in issue, a witness qualified as an expert by knowledge, skill, experience, training, or education, may testify thereto in the form of an opinion or otherwise, if (1) the testimony is based upon sufficient facts or data, (2) the testimony is the product of reliable principles and methods, and (3) the witness has applied the principles and methods reliably to the facts of the case.

Rule 703. Bases of Opinion Testimony by Experts

The facts or data in the particular case upon which an expert bases an opinion or inference may be those perceived by or made known to the expert at or before the hearing. If of a type reasonably relied upon by experts in the particular field in forming opinions or inferences upon the subject, the facts or data need not be admissible in evidence in order for the opinion or inference to be admitted. Facts or data that are otherwise inadmissible shall not be disclosed to the jury by the proponent of the opinion or inference unless the court determines that their probative value in assisting the jury to evaluate the expert's opinion substantially outweighs their prejudicial effect.

Rule 704. Opinion on Ultimate Issue

(a) Except as provided in subdivision (b), testimony in the form of an opinion or inference otherwise admissible is not objectionable because it embraces an ultimate issue to be decided by the trier of fact.

(b) No expert witness testifying with respect to the mental state or condition of a defendant in a criminal case may state an opinion or inference as to whether the defendant did or did not have the mental state or condition constituting an element of the crime charged or of a defense thereto. Such ultimate issues are matters for the trier of fact alone.

Rule 705. Disclosure of Facts or Data Underlying Expert Opinion

The expert may testify in terms of opinion or inference and give reasons therefor without first testifying to the underlying facts or data, unless the court requires otherwise. The expert may in any event be required to disclose the underlying facts or data on cross-examination.

Rule 706. Court Appointed Experts

(a) Appointment. The court may on its own motion or on the motion of any party enter an order to show cause why expert witnesses should not be appointed, and may request the parties to submit nominations. The court may appoint any expert witnesses agreed upon by the parties, and may appoint expert witnesses of its own selection. An expert witness shall not be appointed by the court unless the witness consents to act. A witness so appointed shall be informed of the witness' duties by the court in writing, a copy of which shall be filed with the clerk, or at a conference in which the parties shall have opportunity to participate. A witness so appointed shall advise the parties of the witness' findings, if any; the witness' deposition may be taken by any party; and the witness may be called to testify by the court or any party. The witness shall be subject to cross-examination by each party, including a party calling the witness.

(b) Compensation. Expert witnesses so appointed are entitled to reasonable compensation in whatever sum the court may allow. The compensation thus fixed is payable from funds which may be provided by law in criminal cases and civil actions and proceedings involving just compensation under the fifth amendment. In other civil actions and proceedings the compensation shall be paid by the parties in such proportion and at such time as the court directs, and thereafter charged in like manner as other costs.

(c) Disclosure of appointment. In the exercise of its discretion, the court may authorize disclosure to the jury of the fact that the court appointed the expert witness.

(d) Parties' experts of own selection. Nothing in this rule limits the parties in calling expert witnesses of their own selection.

About the Author

Cecil C. Kuhne III is a litigator in the Dallas office of Fulbright & Jaworski L.L.P., where his practice deals primarily with commercial and product liability matters.

Index